REFLECTIONS OF
PEARL HARBOR

REFLECTIONS OF
PEARL HARBOR

AN ORAL HISTORY OF DECEMBER 7, 1941

K. D. RICHARDSON

FOREWORD BY PAUL STILLWELL

Westport, Connecticut
London

Library of Congress Cataloging-in-Publication Data

Richardson, K. D. (Kent D.), 1958–
    Reflections of Pearl Harbor : an oral history of December 7, 1941 / K.D.
  Richardson ; foreword by Paul Stillwell.
        p.   cm.
    Includes bibliographical references and index.
    ISBN 0–275–98516–4 (alk. paper)
    1. Pearl Harbor (Hawaii), Attack on, 1941.   2. World War, 1939–1945—Personal
  narratives, American.   3. World War, 1939–1945—United States.   I. Title.
  D767.92.R55   2005
  940.53'73—dc22   2004022507

British Library Cataloguing in Publication Data is available.

Library of Congress Catalog Card Number: 2004022507
ISBN: 0–275–98516–4

First published in 2005

Praeger Publishers, 88 Post Road West, Westport, CT 06881
An imprint of Greenwood Publishing Group, Inc.
www.praeger.com

Printed in the United States of America

The paper used in this book complies with the
Permanent Paper Standard issued by the National
Information Standards Organization (Z39.48–1984).

10 9 8 7 6 5 4 3 2 1

Copyright Acknowledgment

The editor and publisher gratefully acknowledge permission for the following material:

Permission granted by Gayle Norris (subject) and Craig Lindvahl (producer) for use of
material from *They Served With Honor*, WILL Public Television Station, The University of
Illinois, Urbana, Illinois, 1995.

Every reasonable effort has been made to trace the owners of copyright materials in this
book, but in some instances this has proven impossible. The editor and publisher will be
glad to receive information leading to more complete acknowledgments in subsequent
printings of the book and in the meantime extend their apologies for any omissions.

CONTENTS

FOREWORD

In the last half century, the widespread use of tape recorders has facilitated the gathering of personal memories to inform us about the past and illuminate our understanding of it. Oral history is an asset because it adds to the store of human knowledge. It supplements the documents and journalistic accounts that were created at the time events took place by adding details and explanations concerning periods in time that may be long past. It can also benefit from the knowledge of what has happened in the intervening years. Something deemed of little consequence at the time may gain a great deal of significance because of developments that took place later. Oral history can also provide a sense of the environment in which things happened—the day-to-day facets of life that people take for granted as they live through them and thus do not bother to record. But those daily events are often considerably different from the way things happen in more modern times and give us a sense of how much things have changed in the intervening years.

One example from the many that are reported in Kent Richardson's fine collection is the matter of delivering and receiving the news. In the past twenty years we have become accustomed to the twenty-four-hour news cycle in which we can get frequent updates from television and the Internet. Technology has brought us to a time when we can see events from around the world as they happen or shortly afterward through videotape.

Sixty years ago, the images were much less available. Radio could provide word pictures and sounds but not the kind of see-it-now coverage that television gives us. Newspapers—except for extra editions—arrived hours after the events took place. Newsreel films were shown in movie theaters, but often with the delay of a week or so, and the scope of coverage was much less thorough than we now experience. Americans in December 1941 had nothing comparable to the coverage of the terrorist attacks of September 2001.

This difference in technology also gave the government much greater control. It was able to censor the news from the world's battlefronts. In 1941, Americans did not really get a sense of how successful the Japanese had been in inflicting damage at Pearl Harbor. Details came only later, when there was also news of wartime success to help shape public opinion.

Pearl Harbor came to be much more than a place in the Pacific or a label used for the Japanese attack on the U.S. warships and the servicemen in the area. It signified a time, a dramatic watershed. History diverged into the pre–Pearl Harbor era of a divided, entanglement-wary nation still at peace, and the post–Pearl Harbor era of a nation suddenly united and ready to confront a foreign enemy.

Isolationism evaporated in a day. An economy that had suffered through the Depression years of the 1930s got a robust burst of energy as contracts for ships, planes, and other weapons flooded into war plants.

Peacetime gender roles had been stereotyped into male heads of household and female housewives, schoolteachers, and secretaries. With men—and often boys—away at war, women moved into nontraditional jobs, and minorities also found new opportunities as the nation's need for manpower grew and grew.

Perversely, the death and destruction of war brought prosperity and led to an era of abundance in the years that followed the war's end. Social consciousness was raised by the absurdity of racial segregation at home during a time when Americans were fighting tyranny abroad.

Oral history gives us a sense of what life was like more than sixty years ago when the scores of ordinary Americans in this book were touched by an extraordinary event. December 7, 1941, was a day that inflicted itself into human consciousness. Though no one's memory is perfect, these stories ring true, for the day of infamy was far more memorable than almost any other. Just as the events in faraway Hawaii influenced millions of American lives, those Americans, in turn, were to have their own influence on events. By their shared sacrifices, willingness to serve, and patriotism, they were able to overturn the ambitions of the nation's enemies. This country has been a different place ever since that day.

Paul Stillwell
Editor, *Air Raid: Pearl Harbor!*
Recollections of a Day of Infamy

PREFACE

Reflections of Pearl Harbor: An Oral History of December 7, 1941, was compiled primarily from replies to more than 1,800 flyers sent out across the United States. The notices were delivered to senior citizens' organizations, VFWs, and retirement communities all across the fifty United States.

Advertisements requesting input were placed in national publications such as *USA TODAY* and the National Council on Aging's magazine. Senior citizens' sites on the Internet were also tapped, yielding approximately 30 percent of my responses.

Some of the replies came in the form of referrals, which then required follow-up telephone conversations. Those dialogues were edited to form, as much as possible, a personal account in that individual's own words.

The remaining 70 percent consisted of direct written replies with only minor edits with respect to spelling and syntax. I wanted each story to reflect the personality of its writer.

Chapter 2, "Impressionable Youth," elicited by far the most vigorous response. That seemed only appropriate, considering that the greatest majority of people who responded were of that age when Pearl Harbor day occurred. Worthwhile and interesting responses fill the following four chapters, with first-person accounts from eyewitnesses, both military and civilian, leading off. Finally, Chapter 7 takes a look at the human toll brought forth from the assault as well as the impending war.

Many thanks go to the multitude of organizations that assisted my efforts by either posting my flyer or passing the notice on to an interested party.

Special thank-yous go to San Franciscan Marvin McDonald, who put me in touch with many of the Hawaiian islanders whose accounts are posted in Chapter 7.

Members of the Pearl Harbor Survivors Association came through in a big way, allowing me a first-hand look at what many of those in the military went through on that December morning many years ago.

My greatest appreciation goes to each individual who took the time to record his or her memories in hopes of informing and teaching those in future generations of a unique period in our country's history.

Some of the personal accounts in this book go into considerable length and detail, while others are brief and to the point. However, each story is a narrative of the times as seen through the eyes of those who lived it. They are the true authors of *Reflections of Pearl Harbor*. Without the efforts of that generation, the United States, as we have come to know it, would have ceased to exist.

This book could be summed up as "a day in the life of America." However, the day was December 7, 1941.

INTRODUCTION

President Franklin D. Roosevelt's message to Congress on December 8, 1941, went as follows:

Yesterday, December 7, 1941—a date which will live in infamy—the United States of America was suddenly and deliberately attacked by naval and air forces of the empire of Japan. The United States was at peace with that nation, and at the solicitation of Japan, was still in conversation with its government and its Emperor looking toward the maintenance of peace in the Pacific. Indeed, one hour after Japanese air squadrons had commenced bombing in Oahu, the Japanese ambassador to the United States and his colleague delivered to the Secretary of State a formal reply to a recent American message. While his reply stated that it seemed useless to continue the existing diplomatic negotiations, it contained no threat or hint of war or armed attack.

It will be recorded that the distance of Hawaii from Japan makes it obvious that the attack was deliberately planned many days or even weeks ago. During the intervening time, the Japanese government had deliberately sought to deceive the United States by false statements and expressions of hope for continued peace.

The attack yesterday on the Hawaiian islands has caused severe damage to American naval and military forces. Very many American lives have been lost. In addition, American ships have been reported torpedoed on the high seas between San Francisco and Honolulu.

Yesterday the Japanese government also launched an attack against Malaya.

Last night Japanese forces attacked Hong Kong.

Last night Japanese forces attacked Guam.

Last night Japanese forces attacked the Philippine Islands.

Last night the Japanese attacked Wake Island.

This morning the Japanese attacked Midway Island.

Japan has, therefore, undertaken a surprise offensive extending throughout the

Pacific area. The facts of yesterday speak for themselves. The people of the United States have already formed their opinions and well understand the implications to the very life and safety of our nation.

As Commander-In-Chief of the Army and Navy, I have directed that all measures be taken for our defense.

Always, we will remember the character of the onslaught against us.

No matter how long it may take us to overcome this premeditated invasion, the American people in their righteous might will win through to absolute victory. I believe I interpret the will of the Congress and of the people when I assert that we will not only defend ourselves to the uttermost, but will make very certain that this form of treachery shall never endanger us again.

Hostilities exist. There is no blinking at the fact that our people, our territory, and our interests are in grave danger.

With confidence in our armed forces—with the unbounding determination of our people—we will gain the inevitable triumph—so help us God.

I ask that the congress declare that since the unprovoked and dastardly attack by Japan on Sunday, December seventh, a state of war has existed between the United States and the Japanese empire.[1]

This is the speech that most Americans equate with the bombing of Pearl Harbor. But it is the day before this address that lingers in the minds of most people who were around during that period.

As the sun rose on that December morning in 1941, most Americans had no idea how the events of the coming day would change their lives and the direction of the world forever.

While Sunday morning was a time for church for many in the forty-eight United States, the residents and military personnel in Hawaii were busy with breakfast or preparing for another fine, yet uneventful day.

Even though most informed people of the world resigned themselves to the fact that America would eventually become involved in what would later become World War II, it was thought that U.S. participation would come in the form of British or European assistance. Few imagined that the United States would be thrust into the war because of an attack on one of its sovereign territories.

While the Japanese assault would indeed be a surprise, U.S. troops had been placed on alert just one week earlier. It should be noted that the United States and Japan had been engaged in peace talks until late November 1941, when the lines of communication finally broke down.

Early on the morning of December 7, the Japanese government began transmitting a fourteen-part encoded message that reached those in charge in Washington, DC, just prior to the scheduled raid. Japan's timing proved to be their only miscalculation of the day, for the attack was well under way by the time the decoded message had cleared official channels.

At two minutes past 7 a.m. Hawaiian time, blips began showing up on

American Army radar just north of Oahu. Radar, a science that was still in its infancy, led those in charge to believe the sightings were B-17s due in from America's West Coast.

The first Japanese bombs fell on Wheeler Field, approximately eight miles from Pearl Harbor, around 7:55 a.m. Hawaiian time. The bombardment continued to nearby Hickam Field where eighteen Air Corps planes were lost.

Finally, Pearl Harbor, which held approximately 100 navy vessels, fell victim to the surprise attack and lost many key ships including the USS *Arizona*. A 1,760-pound bomb crashed through the ship's deck, igniting onboard ammunition that in turn took the lives of more than 1,100 navy personnel. In all, more than 2,300 American servicemen and sixty-eight civilians perished in the December 1941 attack. That assault became the stepping-stone for America's involvement in World War II. One week later, Germany and Italy declared war on the United States, and thus, the lives of virtually every American and others around the world changed due to events that climaxed on that one morning.

"If you were at least four years old in November of 1963, you will never forget where you were when you heard the news that President Kennedy had been shot," wrote Abigail Van Buren in her book, *Where Were You When President Kennedy Was Shot?* (1993). At that time, this author was five-years-old and I am sorry to say that I have little or no recollection of that event. It is a great personal loss to miss one of the most significant happenings of a generation, regardless of whether it's a calamity or a blessing.

In late 1929, the American stock market crashed, taking with it many jobs, monetary assets, personal hopes, and dreams. The 1960s brought us the tragic loss of a much revered president. All other events of the twentieth century pale by comparison.

Late in 1999, in a nonscientific survey by *USA Weekend* and the Newseum, the news museum in Arlington, Virginia, more than 36,000 ballots listed the Japanese attack on Pearl Harbor as the second leading news story of the twentieth century.[2] It will always be one of those events that is indelibly burned into the memory of the populace who lived through that period of our nation's history.

Memories of that tragic event should never be forgotten, even when those who lived through that period are no longer around to recount their stories and detail where they were and what they were doing when they heard the news on that fateful day. For that reason, I decided to collect the personal recollections from those participants and record them here for the benefit of future generations.

On December 7, 1941, my mother was fourteen-years-old and had taken a walk to a neighborhood market for, she guesses, some candy or other such treat. She heard the news over the store's radio and promptly raced home. She went in and woke her mother who had settled down for an early afternoon nap. Her mother began to cry, for she had two draft-age sons.

My father was on his way home from church in the family car when the news broke across the vehicle's radio. Just then he spotted a couple, family friends, most likely on their way home from a Sunday service as well. He pulled over and shouted the news to them. They were speechless.

At that moment, two people relating devastating news changed three lives forever. That couple on the street would always recall that a lad of sixteen broke the shattering news to them about the beginning of World War II. And, a mother would always remember being roused from a peaceful sleep only to hear her teenaged daughter give her the news she had feared for some time. And so goes all that we do in life. Every action is recorded and accompanied by an equal response.

President Roosevelt announced on December 8, that "December 7, 1941—[was] a date which will live in infamy." The following pages document that time has not been able to dull such a powerful memory. The clarity with which people were able to recall that event and the accompanying details more than a half-century later confirms that Pearl Harbor day has indeed become a date that lives in infamy.

1

EYEWITNESS TO TRAGEDY

In 1941, total Allied troop strength in the entire Pacific region numbered somewhere around 350,000.[1] Air power in that region was considered weak and generally out of date. The Hawaiian Islands were no exception.

Pearl Harbor provided the perfect target for Japan's aggression toward Western powers. The islands housed between a quarter- and a half-million people.[2] Oahu was, of course, much less populated in the 1940s than it is today. Sugar cane fields dotted the landscape around the harbor's grounds, which made for an easier line of sight.

Situated directly in the center of the waterway was Ford Island, leaving only two narrow lanes of exit. Block them off, and the port would be sealed.

The aircraft at Wheeler Field consisted of fifty-two Curtiss class planes still in commission, P-40s; twenty older-model P-36s; and less than a dozen P-26s. Most of the older aircraft would not have been competitive with the Japanese Zeros.[3]

At Hickam Field, the aircraft were considered even less valuable in terms of their capability of providing an effective defense. The fleet was considered too slow and too few in number to provide useful protection on such short notice.[4]

Bellows Field to the east was the most basic of airfields. The grounds consisted of a few aircraft and an unpaved strip that was used mainly for emergency landings and training.[5]

Surprisingly, Pearl's facilities were considered new and up-to-date by the day's standards. Those in charge simply had not prepared for an attack of any magnitude.

In November 1941, Japan began amassing their military forces on the remote island of Kunashiri in preparation for a week-long voyage that would bring them within several hundred miles of Oahu. Their plans had been meticulously prepared.

At 7:15 a.m. Hawaiian time, forty minutes before the attack at Pearl Harbor, a large blip appeared on what was then a relatively new, but still primitive technology called radar. Army Air Corps Lt. Kermit Tyler was informed that a blip, 137 miles out and closing from the north, had appeared on a screen stationed at Oahu's north shore.

A squadron of B-17s from the mainland were due in around this time. A pilot had once told Tyler that when aircraft were arriving from the United States, radio station KGMB played uninterrupted Hawaiian music for the pilots as a signal for them to home in on. That morning, Tyler heard the music and dismissed the warning. And the music played on.

ROBERT E. THOMAS JR.

On December 6, 1941, I spent the day supervising the sailors as they unloaded the USS *Nevada*'s main powder magazine. By 4 p.m. or so, they had completed the job.

On the morning of December 7, 1941, the reverberating clang of the general quarters alarm followed by the loudspeaker announcement, "General Quarters! General Quarters! All hands man your Battle Stations!" brought me wide awake. We were being bombed! "This is no drill!" I heard a distant rumble of explosions, turned to my roommate, Ens. John Landreth and said, "Let's go Sandy, this is it!"

As officer in charge of the starboard antiaircraft battery on the USS *Nevada*, I had to climb three decks to my station. I fought my way up through closing doors and hatches as damage control teams buttoned up the ship. I found my guns fully manned but no ammo. I had to single-handedly break open the ammo ready lockers. As I readied myself, I found that our sound-powered phones connecting me to Ens. Joe Taussig were out. Joe had been hit. After failing to receive any response from central fire control I ordered, "Commence firing!" All guns were soon roaring.

Overhead were flights of high-level bombers coming down battleship row. As I watched, the USS *Arizona*, just 300 feet ahead of us, erupted in an enormous flash and thunderous blast that knocked me twenty feet backwards and on to my back. I knew that German and British ships could explode, but couldn't believe that an American ship could blow up like that. It was heart wrenching to see the few tattered survivors abandon ship.

Some time later, the USS *Nevada* began to move as the chief quartermaster took the controls in an attempt to get to sea where we could maneuver and fight. There were no senior officers on board. They were all on land. The *Nevada*, which usually took three hours to achieve full steam, was able to move slowly under its own power in a half hour and was eventually run aground to avoid sinking and blocking the channel. My battery suffered heavy casualties. As we passed the *Arizona*, I realized that I had never experienced anything as hot in all of my life—before or after. That's coming from a man who would later find himself just 2,000 yards from a nuclear bomb test in Nevada in 1953.

As we cleared the burning *Arizona*, the harbor became visible to us. Good God! The *West Virginia* was awash and burning, the *Oklahoma* had capsized, the *California* was listing and afire, and the *Pennsylvania*, in dry dock, was burning. I thought, "We are the only ones left!"

As we passed down the channel, I heard a shout, "Dive bombers! Dive bombers!" I looked up and saw them in an echelon formation beginning to peel off and then down they came. We were their targets. Through our firing they came, the pilots and other details clearly visible. Each carried a single bomb lodged between its fixed-wheel landing gear. As each bomb was released, I could tell from the relative motion as to whether it would be a hit or a miss. The first two or three missed just starboard. The next bomber released and his bomb just grew larger. I knew it was a hit. I said to myself, "Mother, I am sorry."

I ordered, "Take cover," and turned my back before the bomb struck. I was engulfed in a storm of blast, fire, smoke and debris. A moment later, I noticed that I was still standing. I looked around to see a large crater in the deck just a few feet away and in the general vicinity of the now empty main-powder magazine. The bodies of my men were strewn about. I spotted one of my shipmates lying near the edge and he was on fire. I took a step towards him and collapsed. That's when I realized that my leg was broken. My right wrist and hand were shot through as well rendering it useless. I then noticed blood spurting from my arms and legs and I couldn't stop the bleeding. That worried me more than the rest of my physical condition.

I crawled over to the edge of the crater and realized that I wasn't able to pull the man to safety. It became a nightmare as I yelled at the top of my lungs to several sailors just a few yards from me on the deck below. Despite their proximity, they couldn't hear me due to the deafening roar of the battle. I rolled down the ladder to the main deck and ordered nearby repairmen to help the wounded and man the guns.

The wounded were eventually boated to shore and the hospital. I recovered to serve a full naval career of twenty-four years. I will always remember the courage of my gun crews, the leadership of Gun Captain Aldolfo Solar, killed in action, and my chief gunner's mate, Pete Linnartz, wounded in action.

That evening, while I was hospitalized, four planes that flew into the harbor were shot down. The sight rivaled anything Disneyland could produce during their nighttime fireworks. Unfortunately we found out that the aircraft were from the USS *Enterprise* and someone on land had an itchy trigger finger. Once the shooting began, everyone joined in.

Due to the number of badly wounded, they waited until December 10th to operate on me. On the evening of the 15th, my father, Captain Robert E. Thomas, CEC, USN, came to see me. He had been ordered to Pearl Harbor to be the top engineer in the 14th Naval District and the head of the Pacific Division Bureau of Yards and Docks. His primary task was to support the navy's war effort.

I saw my father only one other time one year later while on leave in San Francisco. In January 1943, Dad escorted Secretary of the Navy Frank Knox to the South Pacific. Dad was then summoned back to the States on a secret mission when his transport went down.

On the evening of December 17, 1941, I was secretly evacuated out on the USS *President Coolidge*. We docked in Oakland, California, on Christmas night. All of our casualties were sent to the hospital at Mare Island to recuperate.

I spent eight months in the hospital recovering. My leg wasn't cooperating as much as the rest of my body and refused to heal properly despite having a portion of armor deck plate and a piece of a copper pot from the galley removed from the wound. In June of 1942, doctors went back in and discovered the cause of my infection and lack of healing. Apparently the blast was so forceful that it blew part of my uniform into my leg and it had wrapped itself around my leg bone. I still have a slight limp to this day but I don't really notice it. I lost some of my hearing in one ear from all of the anti-aircraft fire onboard.

The *Nevada* was a gallant ship. Repaired, she fought at Normandy Beach on D-Day and at Okinawa. Finally she was sent to the bottom after A-bomb tests at Bikini in 1946.

I was awarded a Purple Heart, Navy Cross, and the Legion of Valor medal.

Oswald S. Tanczos

I was on mess duty that awful morning setting up tables for the noon meal a few minutes before 8:00 a.m., I believe, when I heard those tremendous explosions coming from Pearl Harbor. About a minute later I heard what sounded like a popping noise, and all at once planes were flying over. I thought it strange, but I continued to finish what I was doing. Then I looked out through the side of the mess hall that was parallel to the airstrip. About 150 to 200 feet away I saw that our aircraft were parked nicely in line alongside the runway.

I looked out through the cheesecloth fly screen and saw black smoke billowing up from one of our planes. As I reached up and pulled loose a corner of the cheesecloth to get a better look, another wave of planes came over from Pearl Harbor about four to five miles east of us. Gunners, firing their machine guns, set fire to more of our planes. I stood there in amazement. What was going on?

I decided to go outside to the front of the building to get a better look. Five or six fellows followed me. From this point on I did a lot of talking—comments, shouts and warnings—but for the life of me I can't remember any of the other guys saying much.

Suddenly, we spotted a fighter plane from the north flying low and slow, just fast enough to stay airborne. As we watched, I believe I said to the other fellows, "That sure looks like olive drab green Army color." My first thought was that the army was pulling a strange maneuver, perhaps a mock attack. Then I noticed the big red ball painted on the plane. "Hey," I said, "that doesn't look like our plane!" Suddenly, I noticed the gunner sitting behind the pilot had spotted us standing in a group. He turned his machine gun toward us. I yelled, "Let's get out of here! I think that guy is going to shoot at us."

We turned and ran to take cover in the mess hall as he sprayed the ground right on our heels. Luckily he didn't hit any of us. This all happened in a few seconds from the moment we caught sight of the aircraft.

When I got back into the building, I took cover under a double sink about six feet long and the bottom about sixteen inches off the floor. I filled the two sinks with six to eight inches of water to deflect any bullets.

As I lay under my shelter, I could hear the bullets cracking and snapping through the building. I noticed the six-by-six-foot refrigerators with about twelve inches of clearance under them. They were arranged in two rows, three back-to-back, and about twelve to fourteen inches between them. I crawled under one of them.

Lying there cramped, I listened to bullets zipping through the building. I could see the feet of five or six men standing squeezed between these refrigerators. I was thinking to myself that these men should not be standing in a line like they were. So I yelled out, "All you guys better not stand in a line like that. If a bullet comes through there, it could get all of you!" They must have thought I made sense because they all moved out. No sooner did they leave then more bullets ripped through the building. When we examined that area later, we noticed that at least two bullets had ricocheted between those refrigerators where these men had stood.

I guess about twenty to thirty minutes had passed since it all started when I heard one of our trucks stopping on the street outside. I said to the guys, "I believe they're dropping off the rifle ammunition." So about six or eight of us went out. Sure enough, there it was. We each picked up a bandolier of ammo, which was about 100 rounds, five to a clip, and walked across the street to our tent where our rifles were hanging on our cots.

When we got out into the street again, one of the fellows was having a problem. I don't know how he got one bullet into the chamber, but there he was with the safety off and swinging the gun around. I grabbed it away from him saying, "If you don't know how to use it, you better get away from us before you kill someone."

Looking at his rifle, I found that in the excitement he forgot to flip the lever that keeps the bolt from coming back to pick up the next round. After I finished loading it, I handed it back to him with an admonishment, "Get lost. Go that way!"

To this day I don't know why I was giving all those orders or took command. The other guys were all about the same rank as I, private first class. Our pay was $21 per month.

Now with my rifle loaded, I told them I was going out where the action was. That's the last I saw of them until chow time at noon. I walked out to a power pole about halfway out to our control tower. This was an old dirigible mooring mast on which we had just built a crow's nest platform with a windsock at the top. I guess I was about fifty to seventy-five feet from our burning planes.

I took my position at this little pole about five or six inches in diameter. I wasn't there long. All at once a bunch of Jap planes from the Pearl Harbor area appeared over the horizon coming straight at me. They seemed to sway from side to side, then opened up with all of their guns. I tell you it sounded like a hailstorm concentrated right on me. White tracer bullets were whizzing by me all around. Some were so close it was like popping a whip at my ear. It shook me up. I felt that I was trapped out there. Bracing my rifle against the power pole to get a better aim, I could get off about three to five shots when they were coming at me, and two or three shots going away. Each time they flew over, I would empty my gun of the five rounds it held.

Don't think I wasn't scared. I guess this was when I started praying for my life. In my simple way I asked the Lord to look after me, and it seemed like immediately I felt at ease or like a shield had come over me. After that I had no fear when I saw and heard all those bullets passing by me.

As I stood there after the first few waves of planes went over us, I thought of an old movie I'd seen about ten years earlier called *Old Glory*. The part that stuck in my mind was the story of a boy born of an immigrant family, like I was. He belonged to a gang that had its own flag, and he died fighting and holding on to that flag. I thought to myself that like him, I felt I would be willing to die for my flag. So as each wave came over, I seemed to draw courage from that thought.

After an hour of this it happened that two groups of planes approached me from different sides, about a half-minute apart. One group of a half dozen or so planes was coming from the east, Pearl Harbor area, and the other group from the north, Schofield area. They had it timed so they wouldn't be over us at the same moment. It's a good thing I decided to shoot at the ones from the east because they seemed to be coming in first.

One plane to the far left was bearing down directly in line with me. When he turned on his guns the incendiary shells were coming out of the propeller shaft at the rate of one per second. These shell shots left a red trail, and I calculated that the fourth one was going to hit me in the right shoulder. I stepped aside to let it pass. It exploded about twenty feet behind me as it hit the ground. Later I found fragments of it which looked as if it were a shell or bullet about one to two inches long and one-half to five-eighths inches in diameter.

The last group of planes came over from the north, the Schofield area. They were so high it was useless to shoot at them. Just as they passed over, I heard a whining, like bombs falling. I decided to lie down and curl up to the pole into a ball to make myself the smallest target. In those few seconds that I thought that bombs were screaming down toward me, my mind raced. My whole life seemed to pass before me in my mind's eye. I was reliving all that had ever happened in my life. Never before or after that have I experienced anything like it.

Again, I came to the conclusion while lying there that if one of those bombs hits me, it would be the end of me. Three of what I thought were bombs hit the ground and exploded, the nearest about 150 feet away from where cars were parked. I found out later they were shells.

The first shell hit and exploded in front of one of the cars and tossed it onto another vehicle. The next shell exploded just outside a round ring of sand built up eight to ten feet high to protect a large fuel storage tank above ground. This was about 300 feet away. Later I learned that someone in a nearby area was shooting antiaircraft shells at the Jap planes flying over us. Instead of the antiaircraft shells hitting the planes or exploding in air, they were falling on us. On top of that, someone goofed. They forgot to arm those shells before they shot them.

After the last of the three shells dropped, I started to shiver and shake. I thought how stupid I had been to put myself into the line of fire! Yet, I felt a certain satisfaction that I had stood up to them and come out of it without a scratch.

I looked around at the ground. It appeared as if someone had raked it. Pieces of limbs from a small tree nearby were scattered around me. I realized then that only the hand of the Lord could have shielded me from all that danger. I made a vow to God at that time that I wouldn't tempt Him again, and I haven't intentionally ever since.

To sum up the casualties and damage we suffered, if I remember correctly, three were killed and three wounded out of some 400 to 500 in my outfit. All the planes at our field were damaged or had burned. None were able to fly. We shot down three Jap planes by rifle fire, and I saw all three go down after I had been shooting at them.

Afterwards I suffered from a strange mix of feelings. Was it all about kill or be killed? Of course, I wasn't the only one shooting at them and that idea gave me some solace. That amazing morning is still vivid in my mind, perhaps because I've told it over and over again for forty years.

DAVE SMITH

After completing boot camp at San Diego, California, I was assigned to the USS *Utah* on November 8, 1939, as apprentice seaman. On the morning of December 7, 1941, I awoke about 7:30 a.m. and left the E-division bunk room, on the switchboard flat, and went up to my locker on the old gun deck. It was one deck below the main deck. I was still in my shorts getting ready to dress for the day. I heard aircraft noise and went to a nearby open porthole. I saw an aircraft flying just off the water coming toward where I was standing. I asked myself at that moment what they were doing on Sunday morning and in port. I thought it must be just another exercise.

I then saw a torpedo drop and the aircraft quickly pulled up. I saw a large red circle painted on the bottom of each wing as the plane climbed to miss our mast. I observed the wake of the torpedo as it came toward me and I felt the shake of my ship as it struck and exploded. I called out to the few shipmates in the compartment that we were under attack by the Japs.

I felt another shudder and could feel the ship start to list to the port side. We had no way to defend ourselves. I decided to make my way to the main deck to find out what we should do. I crawled most of the time up the ladder to the passageway from the port side, past the ships' store to the starboard air castle, and all on my hands and knees.

When I arrived at the main deck where the harbor could be seen, it appeared that the mooring lines were going to hold as the listing momentarily stopped. I could see the battleships on the other side of Ford Island taking hits, blowing up, and burning. Commander Isquith was there and said for everyone to put on a life jacket and prepare to abandon ship. I looked over the side and decided that it would be better to swim under water to Ford Island due to strafing and oil that was spilling from our ruptured fuel tanks. At this time I saw the mooring lines part due to the weight of the sea water that was entering the hull. I noticed a shipmate that was using the lines to cross over to the mooring pilings. He was flung into the air as the lines broke.

I stepped back and took off the life jacket and slid down the side of the ship as it was rolling over. When I reached the island and looked back, all I saw was the bottom of the *Utah*.

During a lull in the attack I went to a nearby base housing unit where a lady was doing what she could to help survivors that were coming from other ships. Some were burned, hurt, and covered with oil. To me she was an angel. She told those of us that were not dressed to go into the quarters and find some clothing. I found a pair of pants, a shirt, and a pair of shoes that I wore for several days. I remember that one sailor came out barefoot wearing a tuxedo.

Tom A. Beasley

I have many memories of my twenty and a-half years in the navy. One thing that I will never forget is the Japanese attack on our ships and out-lying military bases at Pearl Harbor. I was stationed on the USS *Oglala*, but was not on board when it was sunk by a torpedo blowing a big hole in the hull. Since I was a student in Mine Warfare School and the ship was going out for a few days, I was left at the naval barracks to attend school. The ship came back around midnight December 6 and was sunk the next morning of the 7th.

On that Sunday morning I was on the second floor of the barracks when there was an explosion that shook the windows. I ran to the nearest win-dow. There were other explosions and black smoke was boiling up from the Ford Island Naval Air Station, with planes diving into the smoke. Then there was the sound of planes coming from the left. They were com-ing in about the same height of the window. I could see the pilots smil-ing and the red ball on the planes with torpedoes underneath. They would drop down within ten feet of the water before dropping their tor-pedoes.

I ran downstairs where I was given a rifle and ammunition. I took these outside and to a ball field where I stood at the end of some bleachers. I was able to safely fire at several planes that seemed close enough to hit. There were many planes, dive bombers, horizontal bombers, and torpedo planes. Their main targets seemed to be the battleships and other larger ships.

I stayed in the ball field all day. They passed the word by megaphone that saboteurs may have poisoned the water supply and that we were to drink only from sealed containers. This would turn out to be untrue.

When it began to get dark, I went back into the barracks. It was now overrun with people whose ships were sunk. I found a place with my back to the wall. About eight o'clock a person came by and said, "Come with me." I was told to leave the gun there.

Outside, about thirty of us marched to the fleet landing and boarded a motor launch. We were taken to the USS *California* to help lighten the ship, as it was listing and likely to turn over. About halfway in the harbor, it seemed that all the guns began shooting at planes coming in. It went on for a few minutes but stopped suddenly. We found out later that it was planes from one of our carriers going into Ford Island.

We worked all night, and around noon the next day I asked the officer in charge when we would eat. I had not eaten anything since the attack the day before. He sent me back on the next boat, and I went to the bar-racks where they had sandwiches and apples. There were large signs to muster the men from the sunken ships. I checked in with the *Oglala* group, then went out to look at my ship. It was on its side with just a small part of the hull out of the water. There were two men injured, but no deaths.

There was a very strong smell of fuel oil as the harbor was covered with it from the damaged and sunken ships. The oil was on fire the day before and it made it very difficult to rescue the people who were in it.

There was actually a rumor that some Japanese had landed wearing blue denim and red armbands, and that they were in the sugar cane fields.

I have memories of other events but they don't compare to this.

JOSEPH T. PAUL

I was fire controlman 2nd class aboard the USS *West Virginia* the latest and most modern of the battleships the United States had at the time. I was sleeping in the plotting room that is the control center for all gun fire systems, especially the main battery of 16-inch guns. I was awakened by a call from the five-inch control director to energize the five-inch A.S. Battery. No sooner had I started throwing switches when I was shaken by a tremendous explosion followed by five or six more in close succession. The ship began to list badly. I tried to make my way up to topside.

I heard water coming in huge amounts above me and the ship began tilting worse and worse. I tried to get back to the plotting room where my friends were figuring that I was not going to get out this way.

As the water continued to rise, someone at the watertight door yelled, "Anyone else?" I yelled right back, "Wait for me!" He said, "Hurry, I have to close the door!"

As I was going back to the door, I had to walk through an oil shower caused by a broken line.

Getting back to the watertight door and covered with oil, he managed to help me get through and closed the door just in time. We were now in a sealed compartment with no air or lights as the ship had lost power right after the torpedoes struck.

One knowledgeable man began counter flooding compartments and soon the ship began to settle on an even keel and rest on the bottom of Pearl Harbor. At this time, I did not know how I was going to get out. Neither did most of the other men.

Everyone seemed perfectly calm, as if this was a routine drill. About an hour or so after the attack began, we realized that there was nothing more anyone could do. The officer in charge told us to abandon the ship.

We went into the control center, which was in the next compartment, and climbed up a ladder inside an escape tube that emptied into the conning tower on the bridge. I thought how lucky I was and how smart the designers of the ship were to install such an escape tube.

When I finally got to top side, I saw what havoc the Japanese had done to Pearl Harbor, all of the ships, and shore-side facilities. Most of the men ran over to the starboard side and managed to get aboard the USS *Tennessee*. I was delayed by smoke and fire and ran to the port side and jumped into the water. I began to swim away from the ship and was making poor progress when it seemed that out of nowhere a motor launch came by and picked me up. We soon left the area because the oil fire was only a few feet away. A man who later became my good friend, John McGoran, was in that boat which picked me up. We renewed our friendship through the Pearl Harbor Survivors Association some twenty years ago.

I ended up at the submarine base where I showered, was issued new clothes, and given a meal and a mattress. I spent the night there and was assigned to the USS *Henley*.

WILLIAM HUGHES

The USS *Utah* was formerly designated as battleship BB-13 and later converted to an aircraft target ship, AG-16. Two torpedoes struck the *Utah*'s port side during the first wave of attacks on December 7, 1941. It quickly flooded and capsized with the loss of fifty-eight sailors who are still entombed within the ship. Attempts were later made to salvage the *Utah* but were stopped after righting the ship to an approximate angle of thirty-eight degrees. There is a small memorial to this ship and its crew on the northwest shore of Ford Island.

Warren Upton and I worked together and we slept in the same compartment on the *Utah*. The only difference between us on the morning of the 7th? He chose a tough way to depart the old "bucket" and I choose what I thought was easier.

Anyway, we were both strafed, we both ended up in the big trench, and later ended up together over at the air station getting dry clothes. I am not entirely clear on all the details, but I do remember a motor launch taking us across the harbor and unloading us on 1010 docks. We ended up on the USS *Argonne*. We worked the same ammo line that night (the first hard work I had done in the navy,) and heard the same firing, etc.

Warren was put on watch in the radio shack. I was not. On December 8th, we both went and pulled ammo out of the old *Utah*'s bottom. On December 9th, I was transferred to the USS *Vireo*, a seagoing minesweeper, to temporarily replace the radioman who caught shrapnel during the attack.

One week later I was assigned to the USS *Saratoga* and it was off to the war. I would not see my good friend Warren Upton nor anyone else from the USS *Utah* until May 1988—some forty-six years later—when we held our first reunion in Salt Lake City.

I did have the satisfaction of being in Tokyo Bay, Sept 2, 1945, for the Japanese surrender, when the pilots who pulled off their dastardly deed on 12–07–1941, had been silenced.

I was a very fortunate individual when you consider the miles and miles and miles of Pacific Ocean I saw between those two dates. The

Saratoga did catch a "sunset" torpedo between Johnson Island and Oahu, yet I was spared the ultimate horror of the war.

I believe that my mind has protected me a lot, in that I do not recall seeing a single man killed or injured in combat in World War II. I cut my foot on some coral while swimming ashore at Pearl, and that was the extent of my physical injuries.

HOWARD ASA PRICE JR.

Born in 1919, I was twenty-years-old when I joined the navy. There weren't a lot of jobs around in 1939. When a cousin of mine, who had been in the navy for fifteen years, came for a visit and roared up in a big new car, I asked if I could join the navy and get on his ship. My cousin said that I could request that after boot camp. He was on the USS *Maryland*.

Right after boot camp and before I could join the crew, I contracted the measles followed by the mumps. Finally, when the *Maryland* returned to Long Beach, California, I was able to join my shipmates.

I started out on the decks but was eventually moved into the supply department.

On Sunday, December 7, 1941, I was in a storekeeper's office reading the funny paper. When everything broke loose, I thought it might be an early morning drill as that wasn't unusual. When I heard and felt the torpedoes hit the USS *Oklahoma*, which was moored alongside the *Maryland*, I ran to my battle station below deck.

My general quarters assignment was to feed ammunition up a conveyor belt to the top deck. But you see, these were planes flying over, and on deck they were throwing 20 mm ammo at them. We were sitting on five-inch shells. We stayed down there with our unusable ammunition way into the night.

Finally, a chief storekeeper called me and told me of all the bombing and ship sinking going on above deck. The *Maryland* took quite a few hits and we lost a handful of crewmen. To make me feel better, I think, he told me of two Japanese aircraft carriers that had been sunk.

After the *Oklahoma* rolled over, some guys from our ship helped cut holes in its hull because we could hear men pecking on the walls inside. They did get several of them out although I don't recall how many exactly.

I didn't know how to feel about the Japanese after the attack for it was as if we were hit in the back of the head. That is, you didn't know where they were coming from nor why they did it. It was a very cowardly move.

In the end, I felt that the United States was justified in dropping the atom bomb. With so many Japanese suicide planes crashing into our ships in the Pacific, they eventually would have lost the war anyway, but at what price?

B. E. (Gene) Merrill

I was a signalman on the USS *West Virginia*. I had been relieved from the 4 a.m. to 8 a.m. watch on the signal bridge and was preparing to go on liberty.

My living quarters were on the second deck forward. The shower I used was located on the main deck, right in the bow. To take a shower I would strip, tie a towel around my waist, slip into my shower thongs, take a bar of soap and a wash rag and go up a ladder from my compartment to the main deck. I would then go forward, through about three compartments to the shower room.

There were about eight or ten others in the shower room. I had finished my shower and was drying myself when the first torpedo struck the ship. There was a muffled explosion causing the ship to shudder. The bow seemed to rise a few feet then settle down. Someone said, "What the hell was that?" Someone else replied that it was probably an explosion in an engine room.

I tied the towel around my waist and proceeded aft toward my quarters. I hadn't gone but a few steps when the second torpedo struck. Almost immediately the PA system sounded general quarters, with a comment from the boatswains mate of the watch, "The God dammed Japs are attacking!" I headed for my battle station, losing the towel, thongs, soap, and washrag.

My battle station did not involve guns. It was a signal station designed to hoist flag signals to the main yardarms in the event the signal bridge was blown away in a sea battle. Obviously my battle station was useless in a battle of this nature, so I volunteered to join a ten-hand rescue party to go below and rescue those wounded by the torpedoes.

I have no idea how many we rescued. With no instructions, each of us used our own discretion. My modus operandi was to quickly examine a body for signs of life. If none was apparent, I moved on to the next one. However, questionable cases I rescued.

I stayed below until the flooding salt water and oil forced me to evacuate. When I emerged to the topside, the battle was over. The ship was sitting on the bottom with a port list and was burning.

At around noon, I left the ship with what I estimate to be the last twenty or twenty-five men able to leave. It was easy for us to leave the ship. We just clambered down about four feet from the port forecastle into a fifty-foot motor launch. The motor launch took us across the channel to the submarine base where we boarded a flatbed truck that took us to the receiving station barracks.

I went into one of the buildings that seemed to be overrun with women wearing Red Cross armbands. I was naked as a newborn chicken, covered with oil, and practically surrounded by these women. Under normal circumstances, I would have been greatly embarrassed, but in this situation, not at all. None of these "angels of mercy" seemed to pay me any attention. Under normal circumstances, I might have been insulted.

Someone directed me to the shower where I spent the better part of an hour scrubbing oil out of every pore of my body. Upon emerging from the shower, once again appearing to be a Caucasian, I was directed to a small-stores issuing room where I was given a new set of dungarees, white hat, shoes, a change of underwear and socks, a toothbrush, toothpaste, a razor, and a ditty bag in which to carry my now worldly possessions. I wandered out, a sailor without a ship, no sleeping quarters, no mess assignment, and no duty station.

I learned that Western Union, set up on the base, had an improvised message center and one could send a telegram at no charge to notify loved ones that they had survived. I sent one to my mother. She received it sometime the following April. Subsequently, she received my letter long before the telegram.

ED CARSTENS

At the time of the attack I was a Fireman 3rd Class on the USS *West Virginia*. It all started thusly. 7:55 a.m. and I was at my muster station alongside turret number 3 waiting for the bugler to sound a call for colors. Facing the channel waters I suddenly saw two aircraft flying low and heading straight for my ship. I thought it was an exercise of sorts as they roared up and away. But then, two other aircraft, also flying low, were heading for my ship. Watching their antics, I saw two objects fall from their craft making a tremendous splash. Suddenly, I spotted two wakes headed for the ship and surmised they were torpedoes. By the time I got the word "torpedoes" out of my mouth, they had hit and exploded.

General quarters was sounded and I headed for my battle station, located on the second deck in the bow section, as a member of a damage control party. After descending to the second deck, I made my way forward on the port side where the torpedoes were exploding. I learned later that we had been hit with eight plus two bomb hits.

By the time I reached my battle station, the ship had begun to list to port. It certainly didn't help that all the portholes were open allowing water to enter and help flood the ship. I arrived at my battle station along with four other crewmen and a warrant officer, and we waited for further orders. But having lost communication with the bridge, we decided to go aft and lend assistance where needed.

Entering the adjacent compartment, we heard a terrific explosion that knocked all of us off our feet, scattering us like tenpins. Going back to the compartment we had left, we found a gaping hole from a bomb hit. Had we not left, I wouldn't be here to write this.

We made our way to sick bay and proceeded to evacuate the lame and disabled. This took the better part of an hour. By the time we got the last man out to safety, we were sloshing in fuel oil that was chest high that had seeped in from ruptured fuel tanks. At this point, I passed out from the fumes and upon recovering, found myself being supported by two shipmates topside. After assuring them that I was able to navigate on my own, they directed me to a launch that was tied up to the bow and told me to get off the ship. Easier said than done, as the second attack wave had arrived and was in the process of finishing the job of destroying as many ships as possible.

In between strafing attacks, I finally made it to the launch in which was a coxswain and a mess attendant who was vomiting his insides out. In an attempt to move the launch and head to land, we discovered the propeller was damaged and of no use. Man the oars, which we did, but to no avail as the current carried us to the already overturned *Oklahoma* resting with her keel up. We made another attempt to head the launch to the submarine base across the channel just as more aircraft were strafing everything in sight, including us. Fortunately, we were not hit, though the bullets were piercing the water on both sides of the launch.

We then spotted a crash boat approaching from the sub base and it cast a line to tow us to dry land. It was then that the realization of what had happened set in and the feeling of fear caused my body to tremble as never before.

After taking a gasoline bath to remove the fuel oil from my body, and getting clean clothes from the lucky bag, I settled down as best I could for three days at which time I received orders to report aboard the USS *New Orleans*, a heavy cruiser. This also was torpedoed in the battle of Tassafaronga in November 1942 and lost its bow. But that is another story. This then is my story.

ALBERT BERGER

I was born on October 17, 1921, and enlisted in the United States Marine Corps in September 1939. I went with my dad to the United States post office on East Fayette Street in Baltimore, Maryland, for my physical examination and personal history. My dad had to go with me to sign for me because I was only seventeen-years-old at the time.

From there I caught a train to Parris Island, South Carolina, for boot camp, then on to the Pacific theater of operation.

After three or four months in San Diego, we were transferred to San Francisco. From there, after seven days on a ship, I ended up in Pearl Harbor. I didn't know where Pearl Harbor was. I never heard of it, you know, I had no idea. So we got to the Marine barracks which were right next to the big army base known as Hickam Field. Hickam was one of the bases heavily bombed on December 7, 1941. We were only separated from the field by a wire fence, as I recall.

As it was still peacetime, it was very pleasant being stationed at Pearl. After a typical Friday afternoon inspection, we were free for the weekend and nearly everybody would leave and go into Honolulu. It didn't help that we had no money. When I enlisted, we made $21 a month. That's nothing now. Even in those days it was nothing.

On the morning of the attack on Pearl Harbor, I was on guard duty guarding the main gate leading into Pearl Harbor. My job was to see that all the civilian workers who were coming and going were authorized to travel through the gates, and I would check their badges as they went through.

I didn't receive liberty that weekend because it was my turn for duty. We went by turns. Quite often we went by alphabet. In other words, it was to be your turn for duty that weekend if your last name was between A and D. I was a B, so I was on duty from 4 a.m. until 8 a.m.

Exactly at 8:00 a.m. that morning we heard airplanes flying over. I looked up and I saw these low-wing silver-colored airplanes with big red circles on the underside of the fuselage. I looked at them and I didn't recognize them at all. I didn't know what that meant. I didn't know the insignias of foreign airplanes at that time.

One of the people at the main gate was a master sergeant we used to call "Gunny" who, in his late forties or early fifties, already had twenty years of service in. I asked him what kind of planes they were. He said they were Japanese because he had seen them while in China with the Marines.

They began dropping their bombs. They came in, waves of airplanes, and were bombing everything they could—all the ships. They came in right over us. I could see the pilots. They were looking right down on us. Being the brave guy that I was, I took my rifle and I started firing at the planes. I also assisted Gunny. They had what was known then as a Browning machine gun. It was a stationery machine gun. He was manning the machine gun and I was trying to help him the best I could.

Just Friday night I commented to one of my comrades, "You know, I've never seen this many ships in the harbor at one time." That had to tell you that the Japanese knew that practically the whole fleet, except the aircraft carriers, was in the navy yard at that time. They probably weren't right in the navy yard, but just outside.

There was a tank farm right next to our gate. The area was filled with fuel storage tanks. They were right next to where I was standing. Had they dropped a bomb on the oil tanks, which I thought they were going to, it would have been curtains for me and everybody around there. Fortunately, it didn't happen that way.

It seemed to me that the attack went on forever, but actually it was only a matter of hours and they were gone. Of course the place was in an uproar. The ships were on fire. I recall seeing the bodies lined up on the pier that came out of the *Arizona*. A lot of them never got out.

After the planes left, they pulled our four 90 mm antiaircraft guns out of the storage sheds and set them up. It was like shutting the barn door after the horse left. So we sat there on the guns for hours and hours because there were all kinds of rumors floating at that time that the Japanese were coming by landing craft into Hawaii and they were going to capture it. If you recall, at that time they were capturing places like the Philippines and all these other places which was Japan's beginning of the war. They were already on their way across the Pacific.

Finally we decided they weren't coming back, so we put everything away and waited around to see what was going to happen.

Everything was in an uproar. I was in such a state of mind, I didn't know if I was coming or going. I had never been in a war. I never before saw bombs dropped or people shooting. This was all new to me. I was a youngster. I was only twenty-years-old. I didn't know how to cope with it, and there was nobody there to tell me how to cope with it. Most of the men were around my age—all young men—with the oldest one around twenty-one or twenty-two-years-old. Of course the officers were older, but they were not much help in calming us down. Actually, we could have used some tranquilizers because that's how bad it was. Seeing the bodies and the fires and everything was traumatizing—a very, very bad time. Fortunately our company didn't have any casualties.

ERNEST M. PHILLIPS

I entered the Marine Corps in November 1940. I first went through Pearl Harbor in February 1941 on the heavy cruiser *Northampton*.

In December 1941, we were with Task Force 16 consisting of the USS *Enterprise*, USS *Salt Lake City*, USS *Chester*, plus some other eight destroyers. We had been to Wake Island to deliver a marine squadron of fighter planes from the *Enterprise*. We had heard the Japanese were holding maneuvers around the island. I saw a dispatch that said if we went there, they thought the Japanese would leave. However, they really didn't leave, they just followed us to Pearl Harbor.

We were due to tie up in Pearl on Saturday, December 6th. We had been practicing towing a carrier when a line snapped and became wrapped around the propeller shaft. We had to send divers over the side to unravel the mess. It was then too late to enter Pearl Harbor. They had submarine netting in place and a dispatch said, "Delay entering Pearl until 10 a.m., December 7th."

About 7 a.m. on the 7th, about three hours before port, we were just maneuvering around and killing time until 10 a.m. Some of the destroyers kept making submarine contacts. According to the dispatches, they said, "You are in error. We do not have any submarines in the area. Please instruct your operators on the proper use of equipment," or words to that effect. The admiral was very put out that they were making the contacts where they shouldn't be.

Right around 8:00 we were called to "general quarters." We were told the Japanese were attacking Pearl Harbor. Of course we had been through these exercises before and assumed this was just another drill. I went up on the gun and took my blanket. I looked around and everyone else was snoozing. We were expecting a "holiday routine" because we usually had a holiday routine on Sundays. Someone made a remark that "They are making it look real today, aren't they?" We could see smoke coming from the harbor. It finally became apparent to us that we were under attack when they started cutting loose the boats.

We started breaking out live ammunition and threw all of our dummy rounds over the sides to make room for the live rounds. There was a man in charge of unlocking the ammunition box, and he wouldn't unlock it until we got the proper form. Finally somebody threatened to hit him over the head with a crowbar. We took the crowbar, pried the lock off, then took the ammunition and put it in its place.

We were not spotted by the Japanese. We weren't that close in. We could see the smoke but couldn't see the harbor. We turned the ship in the other direction. Occasionally, we could see a plane shot down and we cheered. We later learned that many of those were our own planes taking off from Hickam Field.

We did have to come in later that night for fuel, and that's when we saw what had happened. The *Enterprise* was slated to tie up next to the *Utah*. That's why the Japanese threw twenty-seven torpedoes into the *Utah*. Their information said that the *Enterprise* would be tied right beside it. Apparently their information was pretty good, but it just wasn't current enough.

On November 30, 1942, the cruiser *Northampton* was hit by two twenty-four-inch torpedoes and sunk in the battle of Tassafaronga, Guadalcanal.

EDWARD L. SOWMAN

My naval career began at the naval recruiting station in Denver, Colorado, in June of 1935. I had just graduated from high school and decided the navy was an option that appealed to me. I passed the physical and was told I would be put on a waiting list since the navy was not in need of a large number of recruits at that time. In mid-September of that year I received a call from the recruiting office advising that a candidate had failed his physical. He said that if I were prepared to leave immediately,

I could have his place in the draft. I said yes and on the 15th of September, 1935, I joined the navy.

In August of 1938 I met a young lady from Salt Lake City, Utah, and on Christmas Day 1938, we were married in Littleton, Colorado, a small city just outside of my hometown of Denver. A short few days together and I was back in San Diego with the squadron preparing for another fleet exercise.

In September of 1939 I was discharged from the navy. We returned to Salt Lake City to make our home. I elected to join the naval reserves and attended meetings one night a month in an unused room of the city's post office. My civilian life was cut short in December 1940 when I was recalled to active duty and directed to report to the naval receiving station in San Francisco. I was a twenty-four-year-old navy radioman when the bombs began to fall on Pearl Harbor, December 7th, 1941.

My ship, the USS *New Orleans*, a heavy cruiser, and her sister ship, the USS *San Francisco*, were tied up across a dock from each other in the navy shipyard when the Japanese made their first attack at 7:55 a.m. on that fateful day. Across the water at another dock in the shipyard was the navy tanker, USS *Ramapo*. She had a deck cargo load of one or two PT boats for delivery to an advance base in the Pacific and was scheduled to leave Monday morning. Both cruisers, *New Orleans* and *San Francisco*, were undergoing machinery repairs and were taking all utilities from the dock, which included water, air, electricity, etc.

I was in the chow line, on the port side of the well deck waiting for breakfast, and many of us in the line remarked about the Airedales (aviators) disturbing our peaceful Sunday morning with practice dive bombing. We didn't know then that both Ford Island and Hickam Field were already under attack.

My first indication that we were under attack was when I saw a Japanese torpedo plane pass on our port side. It was close enough that I could see the red ball and the grinning faces of the occupants. This observation coincided with the sound of "General quarters! All hands man your battle stations! This is no drill!" Breakfast was forgotten and I ran to my battle station in the upper superstructure, located three decks above and aft of the airplane hanger.

I was the radio operator in secondary control. Secondary control was an emergency space, where control of the ship could be taken in case of casualty to the main control in the forward bridge area. We couldn't get into the space because of a padlock on the entry hatch, so I took shelter behind a gun tub until the lock was broken off. I tell people, "I tried to dig a fox hole in a piece of one-half-inch armor."

We had had a field day on Friday, in preparation for a captain's inspection on Saturday. This control station, unused during in-port periods, had been secured following the last inspection and padlocked to insure it would not be used as a hangout during the coming week. This kept the compartment cleaner's workload down when the next inspection came around. From this vantage point I watched the Pacific war begin.

Five hundred yards off our starboard quarter, along battleship row, I saw the *Oklahoma* turn over, the *West Virginia* break up mid-ship, the *Arizona* sink into its watery grave, and watched the harbor burn from leaking fuel and debris. I saw whale boats and launches, guided by their heroic coxswains, running through the burning oil and debris to rescue survivors. Oh, there were so many acts of heroism and so little recognition.

Our antiaircraft battery had begun firing immediately after being manned, but suddenly all power from the dock was cut off and the gunners had to go to local control. This meant they would aim and fire from the mount itself without any additional assistance. At the same time it meant that the ammunition hoist would not operate, and on deck ammunition was in limited supply.

Crews were quickly assembled to form a human chain, and passed ammunition from the magazines, deep in the bowels of the ship, to the weather decks where the guns were located. Our chaplain walked along this line of struggling, sweating men, urging them on. With a slap on the back he said, "Praise the Lord and pass the ammunition."

Chaplain Forgy's words went on to become an oft-repeated phrase and later became the title of a song by Frank Loesser. Loesser's song seemed to indict the chaplain, however, because it inferred he manned a gun himself. This was not true. He was truly a noncombatant and lived up to his stripes of a Protestant chaplain.

Later on, Chaplain Forgy wrote a book of his experiences aboard the *New Orleans*. It was titled *And Pass the Ammunition*. Our ship suffered minimal damage during the initial and second attacks, and so, in a few days the shipyard personnel and our crew were busy making emergency repairs so we could get under way. On Christmas Eve, 1941, we were under way with convoy duty.

CARL SCHMITZ

I joined the navy in February 1941. In June I was assigned to the USS *Curtiss* in San Diego. We sailed to Pearl Harbor via Long Beach. I was then assigned to the USS *Castor* (KS-1) as an apprentice seaman. The *Castor* was a floating hardware store. My duty on December 7th was mess cooking for the chief petty officers, which I hated doing. Their quarters were on the port (left) side. That is what I was doing when the general quarters alarm sounded.

My station was on the flying bridge as the captain's orderly. I left the chief's quarters and had to climb cables fastened outside the bulkheads because the ladders had been taken down for maintenance. As I climbed, I looked up and saw planes diving at us. They looked like our SBDs, or Smart Battery Data planes, until I saw the "meatballs" on the underside of the wings.

I kept climbing until I reached my station and the captain handed me a pair of binoculars, telling me to state what I saw. I looked aft and saw torpedo planes crossing our fantail. Two planes passed by, but the third was shot out of the sky. Our gunners hit the torpedo plane and blew it up. I could see three people in the cockpit, the middle one had buck teeth.

All this time fuel was coming aboard. The men assigned to unload the fuel covered up as much of the ammo as they could, then disappeared. Looking out through the binoculars, I saw the USS *Shaw* blown up, losing its bow. I saw high-level bombers flying across the harbor. Planes began dropping what looked like little black dots. I informed the skipper, not realizing they could be meant for us. I followed the "dots" down where the USS *Arizona* lay. The bombs disappeared for a second behind a building rooftop, and then a big explosion arose with fire into the air at least 400 feet high. Our ship, with all of its ammo cargo, escaped with only some pieces of its guns knocked off.

The USS *Neosho* was tied up aft of us loaded with aviation fuel. I am asked if I was scared. I wasn't until night when our carrier planes tried to land on Ford Island and the sky was lit up like the 4th of July by gunfire. Then the sky turned so dark you had a hard time seeing ten feet in front of you.

After a tour of the Pacific, including the battle of Okinawa, I was finally discharged and went to work for the Santa Fe Railroad until I retired after thirty-nine years.

VINCENT A. SCHARFEN

I was born January 4, 1917, in Albion, Nebraska. I joined the navy June 12, 1939, in Boise, Idaho, and was sworn in at Salt Lake City, Utah. I went to Hawaii on the *Cimarron*, a tanker with the 4th Division, and was assigned to a fourteen-inch gun on the USS *Pennsylvania*.

On Saturday, December 6, there was a battle of bands concert, and the band from the *Pennsylvania* won the competition. After breakfast on the morning of the 7th, I was on the dock using the head because the USS *Pennsylvania* was in dry dock number 1. I immediately hurried to my station when the attack began.

We loaded the aft gun and waited but saw no action. Then we unloaded and returned topside since we did not know what we could do. We then manned the lines because the navy yard had started to flood the dry dock. The navy yard command was afraid that the Japs would put a torpedo into the dry dock gate and that it would have caused the *Pennsylvania* more damage.

Ever so often we would be strafed by the Jap planes and would have to go for cover. During the second wave, the *Cassin* and *Downes*, two destroyers that were ahead of the *Pennsylvania* in dry dock, received bombs that were meant for the *Pennsylvania*. They were nothing but scrap metal after it was over.

Many of the sailors and marines on the battleships and other damaged vessels tried to escape by going into the water. Because of the fuel and oil spills from the damaged ships, the water was on fire and many of these men were severely burned if not killed, even when they tried to go underwater. It was horrible.

The USS *Pennsylvania* did sustain some damage but mainly from the flying debris from the *Cassin* and *Downes*. We were fortunate and were in San Francisco for refitting twenty-one days after the attack.

Harley Eppler

I, Harley Eppler, enlisted in the navy in Omaha, Nebraska, September 27, 1940. I was sent to Naval Training Station Great Lakes, for training. After completing training I was assigned to the USS *Vestal* at Pearl Harbor.

The *Vestal* was a repair ship, and after several months I was assigned to the foundry as a molder striker. Here I was in Pearl Harbor, Hawaii, learning a trade, fireman first class, making good money, and all was well with the world. Then came 7 December 1941.

The *Vestal* was alongside the USS *Arizona* when the *Arizona* was blown up. The *Vestal* was hit twice, got away from the *Arizona*, and beached at McGrew's Point.

Later in the afternoon of the 7th, I was sent with our landing force to Aiea to help the army man some antiaircraft guns. I returned to the *Vestal* the next day. The following is the ship's log recordings for the USS *Vestal* on December 7th 1941:

0-400 hours—Moored port side to ARIZONA's port side in berth F-7 in 7 fathoms of water with standard mooring lines in use. #3 boiler in use for auxiliary purposes. Naval ships present: SubBase (CinCPAC-SOPA), ARGONNE (Compass for) and various other units of the US Pacific Fleet. 4 to 8 & 8 to 12 moored as before.

0730 DOWNEY, F. G., 201 02 61, C.M. Smith returned aboard from ten days leave.

0755 Surprise air attack by Japanese planes. Sounded general quarters.

0800 All guns manned including 30 caliber machine guns.

0805 Opened fire with 3" A.A. and machine guns. Japanese planes were bombers and torpedo planes. Their main objective in the harbor appeared to be the battleships. VESTAL struck by bomb at frame 110 port side, a second hit at frame 44 starboard side. Each hit killed one man and injured several. They apparently punctured the ship. The first bomb struck at frame 44 starboard side, starting a fire in G.S.K. lower hold. The fire parties fought this and additional smaller fires started in various parts of the ship by debris from the ARIZONA. At least six torpedoes were counted which apparently hit the WEST VIRGINIA and OKLAHOMA moored in berths astern of the VESTAL.

0820 One torpedo passed astern of this vessel and apparently hit the ARIZONA in the bow that extended beyond the VESTAL's stern. Observed direct bomb hit in a forward turret of the ARIZONA. These were followed by an explosion in her forward magazine. This explosion started fires aft and amidships on the VESTAL.

0830 ARIZONA was observed to be settling and fuel oil on the water between ARIZONA and VESTAL was ignited. VESTAL's after lines parted, making preparations for getting underway.

0845 Cut forward lines. Underway on both engines, no steering gear. Tug pulled VESTAL's bow away from the ARIZONA. VESTAL started to list to starboard and taking water aft. Shipfitter and Blacksmith shop filling with water.

0910 Maneuvered to position S.E. of McGrew's Point bearing 30 degrees distance 910 yards, 35 feet water. Extinguished all fires except in G.S.K. lower hold.

0945 Ship settling. Draft increased to 27 draft the list to starboard gradually increasing, decided to ground ship. Underway and maneuvered to position with Old Aiea Railroad Station bearing 73 degrees T and W. tangent of McGrew's Point bearing 320 degrees T. #2 whitespar close alongside amidship starboard side. Dropped anchor underfoot. Ship resting in mud, ship's heard 92 degrees T. Depth of water forward 11 feet, amidships 18 feet, aft 27 feet. Draft forward 15 feet, aft 27 feet. Casualties: dead identified: Duane, W., USN, killed when bomb struck forward, Reid, W.H., USN, killed when bomb struck aft. Three unidentified, one on 3" A.A. platform and two on stern of VESTAL. Those men may have been either the ARIZONA personnel blown over or VESTAL personnel so badly burned as to be unable to identify. Additional personnel may be lost at time of explosion of ARIZONA's forward magazine. Some men were blown over the side and some jumped. The majority were picked up. An accurate check of all personnel cannot be made until the return of all hands from ashore. Unable to determine the full extent of damage until return of divers now employed ashore. The fire in the G.S.K. lower hold, compartment A-9, the after bulkhead of which is the forward bulkhead of the forward magazine, compartment A-6-M, raised the temperature of the magazine. An attempt was made to remove the powder. Thirty-seven charges were removed when the fumes became so strong that removal had to be discontinued. Three men were overcome, necessitating removal of two to the SOLACE after administering first aid.

1000 Pay Clerk L. Webb, USN, reported on board from 8 days leave.

1115 Flooded forward magazine. ADDENDA to 8-12 watch. 12 to 16 Beached as before.

1405 General quarters. 1435 Transferred five bodies to 1010 dock, Reid, Duane, and 3 unidentified bodies. Flooded magazines A-5-M, A-6-M and A-7-M because of severe fire in G.S.K. storerooms A-9 and A-14 ½ caused by bomb in it. 16 to 20 beached as before.

1610 Set condition TWO.

1615 Fire still burning in G.S.K. lower hold. Flooded forward magazine. 20 to 24 Beached as before.

2110 Air raid alarm, crew at general quarters.

2115 Ceased firing. 2130 Set condition TWO (A.A. gun, machine guns and #3 5" gun manned). /s/ A. E. RICHARDS Lieutenant, U.S.N.R.

In March, 1942, I was transferred to Naval Operating Base Norfolk, VA, to be assigned to the USS *Thomas Stone*. Before going to the Stone we had to take amphibious training. I was in the very first class on the East Coast to get this schooling.

H. THOMAS YANDLE

December 7, 1941, is a date that will forever be etched in the memory of those who survived the devastating Sunday morning attack by the Japanese on Pearl Harbor. In the eyes of a then twenty-two-year-old, vivid images have not been dulled by the passing years.

I was stationed at Hickam Field, located adjacent to Pearl Harbor and separated only by a security boundary. At 7:55 a.m., personnel who were not on duty assignments planned to sleep and otherwise enjoy a day off. Those plans were abruptly changed with the sound of bomb explosions and machine gun fire that literally jarred the foundation of the two-story wood barrack building in which I was located. I was still in my bunk on the second floor when a hail of machine-gun bullets penetrated the roof and quickly got my attention. Along with many others, our building was evacuated as we all looked skyward to find out what was happening.

The thought occurred to us that perhaps the navy was conducting training maneuvers, which they often did, and had missed their target. This notion was quickly dismissed when several low-flying fighter planes, with large round orange insignias on the underside of the wings, confirmed they were Japanese and we indeed were under attack.

I could not see Pearl Harbor from the ground outside our building complex, but I could hear the bombs exploding as if they were in the next block.

All personnel were trained in any emergency to report to their duty station. My assignment at Hickam Field was with the Army Airways Communication System squadron (A.A.C.S.), which was to maintain point-to-point and air-to-ground signal and voice communication. This was provided by the Seventh Air Force to which our squadron was attached. My duty station was located in the fifty-foot-high, air traffic control tower. This multi-floored masonry structure housed various A.A.C.S. administrative offices. The building, topped on all sides with a total glass enclosure, was used by the air traffic controllers. From the tower floor, I could get a clear panoramic view of Pearl Harbor, which was less than a mile away.

I decided to make my way through the housing complex and the base parade field to the control tower which was located adjacent to the main runways and multi-hangar maintenance buildings. Upon reaching the building, I made my way to the tower floor hoping to assist in any way needed as directed by the duty officer. By this time, the attack of approximately forty fighter planes was in full force. Some planes circled while others delivered their bombs, and still others dropped low-level torpedoes to the broadside of the moored ships. The planes executed this attack with precision and seemingly little opposition.

Hickam Field, by now, was under a strong attack to the planes parked off the runways as well as the hangar buildings on the base. The nearest hangar building was less than 300 yards from the tower, and as each bomb fell, the operators would hit the floor, taking inventory of any damage, while the building jarred and shook from the explosions.

Nearly all of the planes at Hickam Field were destroyed and the runways were rendered useless from bomb craters. From the tower I could clearly see all the ships in Pearl Harbor, including battleship row, where at least seven ships were moored in a row, side by side. Other ships, cruisers, destroyers, and tenders were moored nearby.

High, billowing plumes of black smoke, sometimes completely enveloping the harbor, could be seen following direct hits on the larger ships. At this time, nothing could be seen on the surface. When the smoke cleared, the harbor would come into view, and bombs would fall as the attack continued. As the planes swarmed over the harbor, I could see the sky filling with black puffs of smoke from the antiaircraft guns. It would seem impossible for any plane to fly through this smoke, but they did with agonizing accuracy.

Toward the end of the first attack, our air traffic controllers were contacted by the flight leader of a group of eighteen B-17s (bombers) being ferried from the U.S. mainland to Hickam Field. They were requesting ground conditions and instructions. All of the incoming planes were unarmed with little fuel left. They were instructed to fly at a maximum altitude until their fuel would dictate an emergency landing. Pearl Harbor, Hickam Field, Wheeler, Schofield, and other bases were under attack, and the pilots could not depend on ground tower assistance due to the conditions of the runways. I do not know the casualty numbers of those planes or their crews.

My specific duty in the A.A.C.S. squadron was to function as a Morse code operator within an island network of five Hawaiian Islands on which military bases were maintained. Within a few minutes of reaching the radio room in the tower, the base commander had issued a complete radio silence order. This order would prevent the enemy from homing in on our signal should the attack be followed up with further military force or actual occupation. This order did not include the air traffic controllers air-to-ground work, since they were assisting as well as they could with the few planes that actually got airborne.

The second attack began after a ten-minute lull. I could see the returning planes approaching about 15,000 feet in broken formations. They began by revisiting the same targets, apparently to insure a total knockout of their objectives. This attack seemed to be of less duration but of equal ferocity. I looked at the landscape and destruction of Hickam Field and Pearl Harbor about 2,000 yards away. It was a feeling of total helplessness. Ships were ablaze, some listing, some were on their sides, a few had only the bow above water. The boats not totally out of commission could be seen slowly getting under way, trying to escape a mortal blow. Emergency stations were quickly set up as ambulances and emergency vehicles, with sirens blaring, could be heard from all directions as they evacuated the wounded to hospitals. I did not dwell long on my personal safety. I felt as if my time had come and there was little, if anything, I could do. I would just go on being scared out of my pants and hope for the best. Some of the attacking planes flew so low past the control tower that the pilots were near eye level as they passed the tower floor.

Looking back over the attacks, many questions come to my mind. Except for some flying shrapnel or misdirected machine gun fire, why was the air traffic control tower the only operational building on the base not hit? Even as the final attack was ending, a lone plane, seemingly on a direct course for the tower at a height of some 200 feet, was hit by a machine gunner set up on the runway. This caused the plane to veer off course and drop what appeared to be a torpedo. It tumbled end over end, missed the tower, and failed to explode. Why? These questions will never be answered, but will always be in the front of my thoughts.

As the final personal cap to one of the most devastating and disastrous attacks in U.S. history, I did, indeed, have thoughts of the anxiety of my family in Charlotte, North Carolina, with their not knowing if I were dead or alive. As a Morse code operator, I had an unusual talent of being able to transmit and receive the code at a fairly high speed. The usual speed was about fifteen words a minute. I could transmit at speeds in excess of forty words per minute and receive at even higher speeds. I could talk in code without the words being written down, as I was able to recognize the sounds of the words as opposed to reading the individual letters.

Prior to the attack, during the early evening hours, to break up the boredom during inactivity, many operators would engage in chitchats with operators on the U.S. mainland when reception was exceptionally good. Now, the radio silence order was in force to prevent possible homing or beaming in of the enemy force. Any break of radio silence could be detected by triangulating monitors and could result in extreme punishment, if caught, regardless of the innocence of the offense.

Some months previously, I had established a "code buddy" relationship with an operator located in San Francisco who could handle code at my speed. We had many conversations to while away the time. The thought occurred to me that I just might get a message to him, and he could relay the message to my family that I was O.K. During the early evening hours of December 7, following the early morning attack, I was seriously considering sending this message: O.K. RS YANDLE RT4 CHARLOTTE N.C. This message was the equivalent of five normal words. The faster operators would use a keying device called a "bug" which was a manually controlled automatic keying unit as opposed to a slower, vertically operated unit. The question was how long it would take me to transmit the message. I decided to time the transmission in practice. I could send it only once and my "code buddy" had to get it right the first time. After several timings, I had the message completed in eight or nine seconds. I was now ready to go, but was the receiver at his station? I energized my transmitter and keyed two "quick dots" and received the same answer which, among operators, means, "I am ready." I decided to wait a few minutes before sending the dots again to be sure there was no airway static. I received the same answer. I felt the monitors could not react in the few seconds required to send the message. I immediately began sending my transmission with flawless accuracy. At the end of a few seconds of deadly silence, I heard a single "dot," which in operator jargon means, "Message received."

Some months later, when overseas APO mail stations were established, I received a letter from my parents telling of the postcard they received from San Francisco and how happy they were to know of my safety.

TONY IANTORNO

I, Anthony (Tony) Iantorno, was in the Long Beach, California, National Guard and my regiment was federalized September 16, 1940. We were sent to Hawaii October 31, 1940, as the 251st Coast Artillery/Anti-Aircraft

Regiment. We were stationed at Hospital Point, Pearl Harbor, to curtail local sabotage. Breakfast at Camp Malakole was at 7:30 a.m., and I was walking back from breakfast with my gun corporal around 8 a.m.

We saw planes coming in overhead. They were so low that I could see the eyes of one of the pilots. We were stunned and then the pilots started strafing. We ran into the barracks to get our rifles and began firing at the torpedo bombers. We shot off about twenty rounds. We then pulled out the .50 caliber machine gun and fired until we ran out of ammo.

We raced to Pearl Harbor with our guns and were strafed by planes along the way. The truck's windshield was blown out. We went to Hospital Point where just fifty yards away the battleship, USS *Nevada* had beached itself. A tug, the *Holga*, was pulling the *Nevada* back.

The marines on the *Nevada* were firing the five-inch guns at the planes. When the guns went off, it knocked us off our feet. My comrades and I waited for more ammo.

Navy crews were picking up bodies from the water. I helped carry fifteen bodies to the hospital where the nurse said to lay them out on the grass outside because they did not have room unless the person was alive and could be saved. Some of the bodies laid there for a day and a half.

Everyone was so keyed up that they shot at six planes from the *Enterprise*, five of which were shot down. There had been a full red-condition alert a week before the bombing but it was considered a false alarm and the ammo was returned to the storage dump. That's why we did not have more ammo available. We were told that the Japanese might attack somewhere in the Pacific but they did not know where.

I spent the next two-and-a-half years in the South Pacific. I was one of the lucky ones.

CHARLES K. KOHNOW

I was born August 3, 1921, in Philadelphia, Pennsylvania, and joined the Marine Corps in 1939. I left for boot camp in December of that year. Being I enlisted on the east coast, my training was on Parris Island, South Carolina.

In 1941, after a stint in Guantanamo Bay, Cuba, we packed up for Pearl Harbor. We arrived on December 1st and moved into the barracks at the naval shipyard at Pearl Harbor. A similar battalion that had just departed for Midway had recently vacated the barracks. We were given liberty for December 6th and 7th, and most of us headed into Honolulu.

I purchased some Christmas cards on Saturday and was sitting at a writing table in the barracks addressing the cards on Sunday morning. I wanted to get them in the mail ASAP because the mail moved slowly then. While sitting there my pants legs started to flutter and I looked through the open door expecting some visible signs of a wind. I also heard loud booming sounds in the distance and thought to myself that is was just like the navy to have target practice on a peaceful Sunday morning.

I went out on the landing of the second floor of the barracks and could see a lot of smoke and heard a lot of noise coming from the harbor area. I determined that this was trouble and hollered to everyone who was there that we had to go to the storeroom for our weapons.

When we got to the storeroom, we had to move a lot of stuff to get to the .50 caliber machine guns in the back. We also had to use fire axes to break into the rifle chests still packed from our trip to Pearl. Our rifles had been stuffed with cosmoline (a heavy oil to keep the sea air from corroding the rifles) and had to be wiped down before using. We hauled the machine guns and our rifles out to the parade grounds so we could get into action.

The Japanese planes had been going over the harbor and dropping their bombs and torpedoes, plus strafing the area, before taking a wide sweeping turn over our parade grounds on their way to the open sea. So that was our immediate action: shoot at the planes flying over. We did hit one, and every December 7th I see a picture of a Zero's wing leaning up against the side of a barracks and I say that was our hit and our barracks.

LARRY KATZ

Where was I on December 7, 1941? I was there. On the night of the 6th of December, I was in downtown Honolulu with two of my shipmates. We could not get a room downtown, so we slept at a locker club called Battleship Max Cohen's Locker Club. It was alongside of the YMCA and across the street from the Black Cat Cafe on Hotel Street. We slept on top of the lockers at Battleship Max.

The next morning we got up around seven, put on our civies, and went across the street for breakfast at the Black Cat Cafe. We were going to Waikiki Beach that Sunday to celebrate my birthday, which was December 4th.

We got as far as the little park, across the way from the YMCA, when all hell broke loose. We did not know what was going on, but saw planes flying above and smoke coming from Pearl Harbor. We thought they were having some sort of exercise.

Just about that time, someone passed us by with a large portable radio and we heard a message that all military personnel were to report back to their stations immediately. Just then, a large window blew out from an explosion.

In two minutes, we changed back into our navy uniforms, ran out and commandeered a cab, then headed back to Ford Island. When we passed

Hickam Field, we heard what sounded like a typewriter clicking. I was on the right side of the cab, turned to my left and looked out the rear window of the cab and saw a plane, with red streaks, coming down the highway heading right for us. I didn't know what it was, but I sure learned in a few seconds that it was a Jap plane strafing us. When he slid to the right to go down to Hickam field to strafe, I saw that big red meatball under the wing and a stripe down its side. The plane also had fixed landing gear with pants over the wheels. I found out later that it was called a Valance, and the stripe was for a pilot who was commander of his group.

Our driver hit a ditch, and the three of us jumped out of the cab and ran to the navy yard, but we couldn't get back to Ford Island. We were on our own and did not know what to do, so we went to the dry-docked *Pennsylvania*, along with two similar destroyers, the *Cassin* and the *Downes*. They had gotten hit, so we helped with the wounded and whatever.

A little while later, the USS *Nevada* was trying to get out of the channel and was hit. Their skipper put it up on the beach so that the channel wouldn't be blocked. You could have heard the roar when he did that. All of us were trying to "push" the ship on to the beach by yelling, "Go, go!"

We finally got back to Ford and what a mess. We lost all of our PBYs (Patrol Bombers, Y class), or mostly all. When I went up to change, the *California* was in front of my barracks. It was hit and sitting on the water line that came over from the main side.

We had to drink pool water, soda pop, beer, or whatever for a few days.

That night, a few of our planes came from the USS *Enterprise*, and I believe we shot them down. Anything that moved was fired upon.

ED TEATS

I, Ed Teats, joined the navy in 1939. I was shipped over to the Hawaiian Islands in November of 1941. I was stationed on Maui and had flown over to Ford Island on December 6 for liberty in Honolulu. My buddies and I were waiting on the dock at Ford Island for the launch to take us to Honolulu for our liberty in the morning of December 7th when the first wave of Japanese planes began their bombing, torpedoing, and strafing.

When the *Arizona* blew, a piece of history landed less than twenty feet from me. The bugle was slightly dented but clearly inscribed with USS *Arizona* on it. I stuffed it in my sea bag and ran to the airfield.

The PBY planes were all in flame. I immediately started to help move the gasoline trucks out of harm's way. The Japanese planes were strafing the personnel, trucks, plus any other equipment.

I hid along the gymnasium wall at one time to keep from being shot. My buddy, Curt Thatcher, received the Navy Cross for his actions that day. He was seen trying to cut loose one of the ships. For three months we were stationed on Ford Island pulling eight on, eight off shifts because we were afraid of another enemy invasion.

I ended up on Guam with Commander Sterling with the air squadron. After five years of active duty, I prepared for discharge on September 1946. It then hit me that I had a piece of history in my sea bag. I had that bugle from the USS *Arizona*. I held on to the instrument for thirty-five years.

In 1981, I contacted the Navy Historical Museum in Washington DC. The curator, retired Admiral John D. H. Kane said that rather than being lost among memorabilia, the bugle would be the highlight of our World War II exhibit. It is encased with a machine gun from a Japanese fighter plane, the sword of an officer aboard the *Arizona*, part of an American flag, and a recruiting poster distributed soon after the attack that implores, "Remember the 7th of December."

BROOKS HENDERSON JR.

I was twenty-one-years-old that December. On December 6, 1941, at 0400 hours, I was walking guard around the dry dock where two destroyers, the *Downes* and the *Cassin*, with the battleship *Pennsylvania*, were in dry dock for repairs. After a while, the hammerhead crane operator approached me and asked, "Why would you need to be walking guard here?" He was puzzled as to why a lone armed guard was present. What good could a solitary sentry do if something happened? This was the beginning of a historical event etched deeply in my memories.

On December 7th, I thought I was going to be off for the rest of the weekend and had planned to spend the night with my cousin, Frank Reed, aboard the battleship USS *Utah*. I was looking forward to the time off because I had just returned from Midway after seven months of fortifying the island. However, my name was on the guard duty roster for Sunday, December 7th, from 0800 to 1200 hours which cancelled my near fatal plans.

I reported for duty at 0745 in front of the marine barracks for color guard at the flag pole. It was a beautiful, warm, sunny, and clear day. No one could possibly imagine what was to follow.

Standing at ease, watching for the flag to go up at the Signal Tower, it was now 0753 hours. Suddenly breaking the silence of the early morning, a dive bomber appeared dropping its first bomb on Ford Island. Pulling out of the dive over Pearl Harbor, it exposed the bottom wings with a red circle on each of them. Following the first bomber came another and another. So began the disastrous onslaught of squadrons of Japanese dive bombers, torpedo planes, and horizontal bombers followed by damage, destruction, death, and horror on Pearl Harbor and Hickam Field.

My main duty was with the 3rd Defense Battalion, Fleet Marine Force. After being released after the colors were posted and the flag raised, I was ordered by the officer of the day to report to my outfit. Joining the ranks of my platoon, we immediately began the procedure of getting antiair-craft weapons, which were housed in gun sheds, into effective action. My personal duty was to set up the three-inch antiaircraft guns while wait-ing for ammunition to arrive. It was being transported by truck from Lu-alei, a naval ammunition depot about eighteen miles away.

I was our platoon's Browning automatic rifleman and now was on the parade field firing at the torpedo and dive bombers coming in from tree-top level as they pulled out of their torpedo runs on the ships in Pearl Harbor. Some were strafing us as they passed over the field. As fast as a friend with me could load the ammunition clips, I was firing at the planes. Along with others who were firing .50 caliber machine guns and other small arms, we saw one plane disintegrate and one plane on fire. The latter plane was so close, we could see the panicked pilot and the gunner struggling to open the canopy to bail out. Another plane, by the sound of the motor, seemed to be out of gas and cracked up by the naval hospital. A friend, Charles Downey, and I ran to the scene of the crash and discovered the body of the pilot lying on the ground. He had been thrown out of the plane. The gunner was still in the plane and was also dead.

On the way to check out the plane by the hospital, the USS *Shaw*, which was in dry dock, blew up and we had to run for cover to escape the falling debris. It all seemed unreal, but one did not have time to think, only react, and do what we had been trained to do. Many of the naval officers were unable to reach their ships for duty and were in tears. They wanted to help so they joined us in setting up our antiaircraft weapons on the pa-rade field.

I was able to keep only one souvenir of the Pearl Harbor attack through the next forty-one months. I remember vividly when this .30 caliber armor-piercing bullet whizzed by my ear and dropped on the ground. It was from a strafing plane, and was so hot that when I tried to pick it up it burned my fingers causing me to drop it. I picked it up when I could, put it in my pocket, and I still have it.

At dusk on December 7th, part of us were moved to Hickam Field where we set up a battery of three inch antiaircraft guns at the Army dump. A few days later, our platoon leader, Captain Stonecliff, volun-teered us to go on a special secret mission. During the night, we loaded onto a four-level destroyer, the USS *Thornton*, and waited until daybreak for the submarine nets to be opened at the entrance of Pearl Harbor so we could leave. We steamed past the ships still smoking in the harbor and the terrible scene of destruction from the Japanese attack.

The captain of the destroyer came down from the bridge as we left the burning destruction and stood among us. I will never forget what he said to us. "I have sealed orders for where we are going. Take a good look around because you may never see this place again. You are standing here with one foot in the grave."

During my time overseas, I stared death in the face many times. More times than I probably even knew, but because of God's protection, I was spared.

EDWARD J. GREANEY

On December 7th, 1941, I was a ten-year-old living with my father in Hawaii at a Koko Head beach house on Oahu. My mother was on a trip to the mainland United States visiting her family and my two college-age sisters.

It was early Sunday morning and my father was preparing for us to go to mass in Kaimuki, at St. Patrick's Church. A neighbor came into our yard from the beach telling us to turn on our radio because we were under attack. I remember he had his German shepherd "Sheba" loping along with him. Father did turn on the radio, but the news didn't deter him from attending mass. As we entered the church, my father stopped to talk briefly with a man he knew who was coming out of an earlier service. This man lived on the mountain heights above Kaimuki and told father of seeing the first wave of Japanese bombers flying over Pearl Harbor shortly after 7 a.m. It was now 9 a.m. When it was time for the sermon, the priest was brief, saying that the pastor had told him to "cut it short" that morning.

My father was a partner in a public accounting firm in downtown Honolulu. He had a corner office on the top (fourth) floor of the Dillingham Transportation Building, which still stands today. After church, we decided to go to his office to see what could be seen towards Pearl Harbor. There were several people already there. I remember Mr. Heu telling me of seeing planes dropping bombs earlier in the morning. At that time (before the age of Honolulu high-rise structures), the Dillingham Building commanded an unobstructed view towards Pearl. We could still see enemy planes in the air there, and the time must have been after 10 a.m.

It soon occurred to father that we were directly across the street from a likely civilian target—Oahu's main power plant. A modern-day generating facility still occupies this site. By coming downtown to rubberneck history in the making, we had indeed placed ourselves in harm's way. He told the others to evacuate and went downstairs to the building garage to reclaim his car. The garage superintendent was on duty. He said he had received orders not to let any cars leave the garage. My father replied, "Well, if I get started, maybe they won't stop us." He wasn't about to stick around and the superintendent really wasn't prepared to stop him either.

When we got to Ala Moana Boulevard by Fort Armstrong, just before the South Street intersection, the car immediately in front of us was hit. We realized later it was undoubtedly an antiaircraft shell fired from the fort. My father's evasive action was to turn left on to South Street. There we passed the Advertising Building (now the News Building). It too had taken a hit from such a shell. A Christmas party for newspaper carriers was in progress, but my recollection is that we learned there were no casualties there. As we went along King Street in the McCully district, however, we could see stores (owned by local Japanese) on fire. We thought at the time that this was ironic, but again these fires were attributed to antiaircraft fire. To this day, when I enter the World War II room of the Judicial History Museum at Hawaii's Supreme Court, I experience a strange feeling because the panoramic photograph of the McCully fires at the room's entrance is an event I vividly recall.

As we proceeded up Harding Avenue, retracing our route from Kaimuki, I was aware of several planes flying high over us and asked my dad whether they were Japanese. He told me they were ours, but afterwards confided to me that he had lied momentarily trying to spare me anxiety.

After we got home to Koko Head, we went over to the house of the neighbor who first alerted us that morning. Standing in his yard, we witnessed a dogfight involving two "rising sun" aircraft and two of our own. The Japanese planes quickly fled, and on the ground we raised a cheer. Recalling these events today, I realize that straggling enemy aircraft must have been in the air over Oahu quite late that morning.

I do remember saying to the neighbor's wife that I heard on the news that a Japanese envoy was supposed to be in Washington, DC, right then to discuss terms for keeping peace between the two countries. She had a few choice cuss words for that gentleman that raised the eyebrows of this ten-year-old.

The war brought profound changes to daily life on Oahu, of course. In the first few chaotic days after the attack, my father and his neighbor friend were pressed into civil defense service "guarding" a bridge across Paiko Lagoon's fishponds near Kuliouou.

These were the days of a *haole* (Caucasian) hegemony in Hawaii, when Caucasians of comfortable circumstances could afford domestic "couples" in their households who were usually Japanese. We were no exception. Teneko was *issei*, or a first generation Japanese American, while her husband, Raymond, was locally born or *nisei*. He was a skilled carpenter but couldn't find work after the mainland Depression of the 1930s took hold in the islands. Their quarters featured a Shinto shrine.

The months of political uncertainty preceding the attack had given them much anxiety. I remember Raymond telling me, the weekend before the attack, that he didn't believe the two countries would go to war. "We are too good of friends for that," he told me. If my father had any reservations about leaving me in their care while he guarded a nearby bridge, he certainly gave no outward sign of it at the time. I really do not believe he ever entertained any doubt of their American loyalty.

This was not the case with all *haoles*, by any means, but it was true of those who influenced my ten-year-old perceptions at the time. Most notable was Mrs. King who lived across Kalanianole Highway on Lunalilo Home Road. She had stepped in to care for my fifth grade class shortly after the attack. Our school grounds had been taken over by the army, so the class met in the home of a local Japanese doctor. She spoke to us fifth graders of the necessity to draw a sharp distinction between the Japanese enemies overseas with whom we were at war and the local Americans of Japanese ancestry.

Mrs. King's distinction wasn't universally shared among our nation's higher officialdom, and several thousand Japanese aliens (ineligible for citizenship) were rounded up throughout the islands. It was not the wholesale internment and evacuation that prevailed across the mainland's West Coast for Japanese aliens and citizens alike—if only because in Hawaii, such a feat would have been logistically daunting.

It is worth noting for the historic record, however, that Caucasian enemy aliens in Hawaii were rounded up as well. One of these was a friend of ours, Mrs. Todd of Pacific Heights. My father and I went to visit the Todd family soon after the attack, possibly because their home had a commanding view of Pearl and Hickam Air Base. I remember looking through their telescope at the burned out hangars at Hickam. Immediately after our visit, Mrs. Todd was picked up by the FBI as an enemy alien of the Italian persuasion. She wasn't held long. It subsequently was determined that while she was of Italian birth and citizenship when she arrived in the Hawaiian kingdom, as an infant she may have become a subject of Queen Liliuokalani's after this and prior to her marriage to a British subject. However, this marriage apparently conveyed at the time British citizenship to her. In any case, her husband had taken the necessary steps to become a naturalized American citizen, although she had not. It was decided that she was, if anything, a British citizen, an allied alien and not an enemy one.

As for Teneko and Raymond, neither were interned. Indeed, Raymond's carpentry skills were now in demand for war mobilization. He became a carpenter crew foreman at Tripler Army Hospital. But shortly after the attack, I triggered an incident that must have given my father pause. He came home one day to be told by Teneko that she found me holding his automatic pistol that he had secured on the top shelf of his clothes closet. I was chastised, but the pistol disappeared for good immediately thereafter.

A great many civilians in a position to do so, both Caucasian and Asian, left Oahu for the mainland as soon as they could following the attack. My mother, on the other hand, was among the first civilian women permitted to return to the territory following the attack, on the first ship to carry civilian passengers to Honolulu, the Kaiser cement vessel *Permanente*. She said she never doubted that we would win the war, so she didn't hesitate to return. I am prepared to be corrected, but my impression is that her return on that historic trip preceded the Battle of Midway. After this American victory at sea, the threat of a Japanese invasion for Hawaii receded.

GENE WHITE

I was twenty-eight-years-old, married, and living in Honolulu then. My father was a captain in the navy stationed at Pearl Harbor. He was on the verge of retirement at that time. We were aware of the hostilities that had been building up between Roosevelt and the Japanese government during the weeks and months before the Pearl Harbor attack. You see, Japan had been throwing its weight around for some time. Their country is made up of a series of islands, largely connected, with a finite set of resources. Washington told them to knock it off, but Japan had reasons for doing what it was doing. Their existence was becoming threatened.

We had been warned by Washington that military action could be a possibility and to keep a look out. However, Japan figured out exactly when they could catch us asleep—literally.

I had gotten up early on the morning of the 7th and had gone over to my father's home around 7:45 a.m. They lived over in another part of the valley. I think I wanted to borrow a gardening tool or something.

My dad came out in his dressing gown with a cup of coffee and a cigarette. As our conversation went on, we heard a "bang! bang!" in the distance. Actually these were antiaircraft guns that we heard. They had been strategically placed around the island, however there was nobody around to man them. Those who did get out there had to take all of the canvas off of them and get them going. What we heard were the first shots they managed to get off.

My father said, "I haven't heard of any maneuvers." We still thought they were running an early morning exercise. He said, "I didn't think they'd have that on Sunday," referring to the early morning practice.

We went to the porch and looked out but couldn't see anything. Right then, the phone rang. He picked up the phone and answered, "Captain White," just like he did at the office. Now, I never heard my father swear, but he then said, "The hell you say!" He then slammed the phone down and ran into the bedroom and began pulling things out of the drawers.

"Hey what's going on?" I asked. He came out of the bedroom pulling on his uniform while strapping on a big .44 around his waist.

About this time, this officer friend of his came screeching up in a Studebaker. He ran out of the house and jumped in. He didn't tell me anything.

I got in my car to go home and turned on my radio to station KGU. There was a minister intoning a drab sermon of some sort. All of a sudden his voice trailed off. I wondered what happened. Webley Edwards, the announcer, came on and said, "We interrupt this broadcast to bring you this important speech. Please pay attention," he said. "The island is under attack! I repeat, the island is under attack!" Then he said it for a third time, "The island is under attack by hostile forces!" Then he said something rather funny. "Don't be alarmed," he said. "We have the situation well in hand." They didn't have anything under control.

I went tearing home and my wife was sitting in the kitchen with her feet up and reading the newspaper. I said, "Hey did you know that the Japanese were sinking all of the ships in Pearl Harbor?"

She didn't answer me. She was busy reading something. I then asked, "Did you hear what I said?" I repeated my question. I had never heard her swear up to that point either.

She then said, "Why those—, I knew they were going to do something like this!"

I said, "If you knew, why didn't you tell somebody?"

Afterwards, we didn't feel scared. We felt more angry than anything else. We kept the radio on and listened all night. Every once in a while, on a military band, we'd hear a voice say, "One high west, unidentified." We thought, "Oh no, here they come again." We heard an occasional "boom" off in the distance afterwards. To this day we don't know what that was.

The days that followed were pretty tense. Martial law was in effect, so every soldier was a policeman. They were very strict about blackouts. One time a Japanese service station owner had left a small light on in a display case and went home for the night. The National Guard couldn't get into his business to turn the light out, so they shot it out. Not surprisingly, the store owner filed no complaint. He knew it was his fault.

One lady was out in her yard and went to light up a cigarette. The light from the match was enough to have her arrested and fined $15. It was either that or give a pint of blood. The island was real short in supply and high in need. She chose to give blood.

We were all issued gas masks and had to get a vaccination for some disease they thought would break out. If you were caught downtown without your gas mask, the MPs would bawl you out and make you go back home and get it.

I wanted to take my wife out to see the *Arizona* several days after the attack. There was a small pier you could drive out on and see the wrecked ships pretty close. You couldn't get into Pearl Harbor at all, so my father got me a pass to the pier. We drove to the gate and produced the pass. We were allowed to proceed. We drove out on the cement pier, and there was the *Arizona*. What a horrible sight.

My wife said, "Take me home. I don't want to see this." One reason was that we heard the stories of men still trapped within the ship. So we turned around and went home.

HELEN GRIFFITH LIVERMONT

I was thirteen-years-old on December 7, 1941, and living in army housing at Schofield Barracks, Ohau, Territory of Hawaii. We lived in the area known as Carter Gate, close to Wheeler Field—home of the P-40s. My dad was the first sergeant of Service Company, 21st Infantry Regiment, and my sister's fiancé was a mechanic on P-40s stationed at Wheeler.

My sister and I were in bed when it all started and discussed how terrible it was to stage a sham battle on a Sunday morning! The noise from the bombs grew louder, so we got up and joined our parents in the kitchen.

My mother was in a frantic state. She was a German war bride of World War I and knew the sound of bombs. She then headed out the door for the "safety" of the concrete housing across from us (ours was made of wood). My sister followed her, and I thought I had better get out too. We lost track of our mother, but my sister and I ran between the houses, dodging bullets for what seemed like an hour! We could even see the pilots of the attacking planes—they were that low! Finally, a lady in one house had us come inside where we stayed until the bombing and shooting stopped. While we were there, we saw my dad head for the baseball field dugout where he stayed until it was over. My mother was safe at another house.

Very shortly after that, there were soldiers all over the place digging trenches in the lawns for us to get into when the next attack came. In the meantime, rumors were flying about ships off shore ready to invade the island, so we were all pretty frightened.

Then word came that women and children were to go to the barracks for safety, which we did. While we were there, there was another attack during which we hid under the beds! Later we were told that women and children were going to be evacuated, so we went home and packed a few more bags and waited. Next we were told to get in the army trucks as we were leaving right now—to where, we had no idea.

After a slow trip filled with no lights, sirens, and bullets flying overhead, we ended up in Honolulu at Kalakaua School. On the way, we could see the ships on fire at Pearl and what a horrible feeling it was! I'm glad I was too young to really understand what was going on there.

The school we went to was full of women and children of all ages, plus an oriental cooking staff which we hoped weren't Japanese. I remember the noise, the smell of citronella used for insect repellent, the crowded conditions, and the fear. We stayed there for a week, not knowing where my dad or future brother-in-law were or how they were. My sister finally got a letter telling her that Jim had a narrow escape, but was O.K.

After that week, they took us back to Schofield and we spent our nights next door where they could black out the homes easier than ours. We had a curfew, of course, and no one wanted to venture out in case the guards mistook us for the enemy!

We were told the women and children would be evacuated to the States. Pregnant women, babies, and small children first. Since we would be last on a long list, we more or less went back to leading a normal life.

I was to get a bicycle (my first) for that Christmas, so I got it early. My girlfriend, a boyfriend, and I really got use out of our bikes during those days. We went everywhere on post, dragging our gas masks along each time. They even arranged for the older kids to take tennis lessons to keep them busy, since there was no school for the rest of the time we were there.

It was a fearful time as rumors were being passed around about the Japanese treatment of women, etc., and we were sure they were going to invade us at any time. My future brother-in-law gave me a knife which I carried everywhere.

Finally, on April 5, 1942, we were put aboard the HMS *Aquitania*, a beautiful luxury liner that had been transformed into a troop ship, for the trip to the United States. We had a cruiser convoy with us for half a day, but since the *Aquitania* was so fast, they decided we could make it on our own.

The trip was anything but pleasant, but the British and Australian sailors were nice to the kids, and we could go anywhere on ship as long as we didn't get in the way of their duties.

We docked in Southern California where the Red Cross ladies met us, fed us, and put us up at a hotel in Long Beach. Luckily, my aunt and uncle lived in Santa Paula, California, so we stayed with them for a while. We later joined a friend to go to Moline, Illinois, then finally on to Minneapolis, Minnesota, where we awaited word from my dad as to his station.

He was given a field commission and transferred to San Francisco, so we met him there to live for the next nine months. Then began the moving process all around the States. We were never in any one place for very long. It was a long war and seemed as if it would never be over, but we survived though many of our men did not.

One of the highlights of my life was the surrender of the Japanese, but it took me a long time to get over the feelings of hatred for their actions, and the terrible attack on Pearl and the airfields.

EMILY GAINS PIPER

Early in the morning of December 7, 1941, we breakfasted with friends who had just arrived on the 7 a.m. interisland boat from the island of Kauai. We heard what we thought was a blasting from a nearby quarry, then realized that it was a bombardment. We commented that they were probably having maneuvers at Hickam Air Field.

As the noise became louder, we climbed a huge mango tree and were astonished at the air battle going on. We were too far away and in the wrong direction to look down upon Pearl Harbor, but we could easily witness the air attack at Hickam Air Force Base. We could see the smoke beyond Pearl Harbor.

Turning on our radio, we heard Webley Edwards, our news commentator, say, "This is the real McCoy. The Japs are attacking Pearl Harbor. Take cover!"

We took to the tree again for a better view. At that moment we saw a plane nearby heading in our direction. Soon it was near enough to see the rising sun emblem. As we watched, we saw the Japanese pilot looking down. It was at that moment that he pulled a lever, and we could see a bomb falling. It seemed that it would drop very close to us so we scrambled down the tree fast. It actually fell several blocks away.

We dashed there to see what damage had resulted. We witnessed a holocaust! Everything was ablaze and we witnessed the first civilian casualties. A Japanese woman had a bomb fragment which had gone through the side of her head and the other side of her face was gone. Her baby died in her arms from a bomb concussion. The owners of the drugstore had perished.

The attack began around 7:55, and the time was now about 8:30. That first attack lasted nearly one hour with four waves of attacks. Pearl Harbor was in utter chaos.

With the imposition of martial law came blackouts as another invasion was expected. The radio gave the news of how our fleet was destroyed and the thousands of men who were doomed on their ships. Those who jumped overboard were often badly burned from burning oil slicks. Only essential personnel were allowed on the street.

The night of December 7 was a nightmare. The news was full of contradictions, and we all knew that a second attack would mean a takeover of the islands. We spent the night listening to the radio to broadcasts of Japanese parachuting at various locations around the island and of landings on other islands (all false).

When the morning of December 8 arrived, it was with relief and disbelief that there had been no further attacks. We went to the University of Hawaii's campus to care for the evacuees.

There was an extreme shortage of blood, so we went to the Queens Hospital to donate blood, as did thousands of others. We will always remember that every lumberyard turned to making coffins, and we saw truckload after truckload leaving these yards for Pearl Harbor.

We were all concerned about our families on the other islands as no telephone service was allowed. No one knew whether the other islands had been hit or even occupied. Finally, on the 9th of December, with strict censorship, we were allowed to call home to say we were okay. Naturally we were cut off and admonished for asking leading questions, but at least we knew there had been no attack at home and everyone was well.

To avoid an epidemic of typhoid, diphtheria, and smallpox, the largest immunization ever undertaken in one area was begun for the 350,000 islanders. Air-raid shelters were constructed everywhere and gas masks were issued. Because of the fear of Japanese occupation, all U.S. currency was stamped with "Hawaii" on it so that it became occupation money and would become useless should an invasion occur.

The navy lost 1,200 men, mostly in the first ten minutes of the attack. The Marines had 109 dead, and the army lost 218. In addition to those numbers, 1,000 were wounded. Sixty-eight civilians died and 35 were wounded. Eighteen of our ships were sunk or badly damaged and 200 planes were destroyed, accounting for a total of 3,630 dead and wounded. The Japanese lost 29 planes, 1 submarine, 5 midget subs, 55 airmen, as well as 60 to 70 navy personnel.

We lived under martial law for many months. A curfew was enforced for three months beginning at 6:00 p.m., then for about one year it was extended to 8:00 p.m., finally the curfew became 10:00 p.m.

We worked seven days a week, ten hours a day. Most university students (everyone sixteen years of age and older worked unless unable to) worked at Pearl Harbor where the need was greatest, and we spent our free time with patients in hospitals. Most rewarding. We wrote letters to families and talked to burn victims who were in such pain.

During the four years of war, we got used to barbed wire closing off the beaches and the influx of thousands of government workers and military personnel on the island of Ohau. In Waikiki, you could look down the main street and see the white hats of sailors on leave as far as you could see.

There were lines for everything. Restaurants closed at 5:00 p.m., beer parlors allowed only two beers, and movies were shown in the afternoon only.

Kodak established the V-mail center and did the microfilming of military letters, which saved tons of mail shipments. All mail was censored.

Our worst memories were the exhumation of temporary graves, bodies being found many months later in the waters of Pearl Harbor, and the burn victims who suffered so much.

The war in the Pacific ended on September 2, 1945, and our greatest thrill was the V-J Day parade. Transportation back to the mainland was at a premium for many months, but by early 1946, most civilians had returned home after serving at Pearl Harbor as well as other defense sites. To the islanders, it was a slow return to a much lazier life at the beaches without barbed wire fences, curfews, and air-raid shelters!

PENNY BELCHER

My father, John J. Belcher, was in the navy and worked in the disbursing office at the USNAS, Kaneohe Bay, Hawaii. He lived at Kaneohe Bay with his wife Lucile and daughters Paula, three, and me, at age eight months. Our plans for that Sunday were to go on a picnic at Diamond Head beach in the morning, and in the afternoon Dad was going to visit two of his friends stationed on the *Arizona*.

He had just gotten up that morning and walked out on the porch to retrieve the Sunday paper when he heard the planes. He thought the navy boys were out very early, but when he looked up at one of them as they passed over the house, he saw the "rising sun" on it and realized they were Japanese planes. He said that they were flying so low that he and a neighbor ran into their houses, grabbed their guns, and actually fired bullets into the aircraft. After the attack, the women and children were sent to a dairy about two miles back in the woods with navy escorts for protection. I'm not sure how long we stayed there but I think Dad said it was two to three days.

My grandparents lived in Columbus, Georgia, and I'm sure they went through torment on that fateful day not knowing whether we were alive or dead. On Wednesday they received a telegram from Daddy and all it said was, "All Okay!" My grandmother said she sat down and cried with relief when she received word that we were all safe.

All the women and children of military personnel were sent back to the United States in February of 1942. I understand that our ship had one or two destroyers for escort and protection. Daddy stayed in Hawaii and was also on other ships in the Pacific later.

Many years following the attack, my sister Paula would not go to sleep at night without a night-light in her room. She was so afraid of the dark and thought the "Japs" would get her. I guessed that stemmed back to having to cover the windows at night after the attack. I was really too young to be affected by it.

JEAN CARLSTON

I was five-years-old and stationed with my parents (my father was army) at Schofield Barracks on December 7, 1941. When the attack was under way, I remember the planes flying over and the empty casings falling on the roof of our house like hail. If the planes had come just a little later, I would have been sitting on the curb waiting for the bus to take me to Sunday school.

My father ran to his office amid bullets, one of which we still have as a piece of shrapnel. My mother, grandmother, and I were evacuated to a barracks across the street right next to the hospital.

There were women, children, dogs, cats, and other family pets packed into this room with a soldier positioned at the window with a rifle. That night we were evacuated under cover of darkness to a native schoolhouse in the hills. The bus went by Pearl Harbor and I still remember the burning ships. I also remember the mosquitoes that tormented us all night in the open schoolhouse where we slept on the floor.

We were on one of the first ships to be sent back to the States on Christmas Day. It was mainly filled with the wounded, but some staff families and navy personnel were sent as well. We went zig-zag during the day, and full speed straight ahead at night in hopes of avoiding any Japanese submarines. We landed in San Francisco on New Year's Eve.

DOROTHY CARLOS

On the morning of December 7th, I was on my way to church when I saw the planes flying overhead. Wahiawa is adjacent to Wheeler Field and Schofield Barracks. I saw the bombs coming down. There were some neighborhood boys also watching and one of them was killed.

I ran into the house and listened to the radio. It was then announced that the Japanese were attacking us. We were ordered to stay indoors. It was unbelievable.

At nighttime, we were not permitted to have any lights turned on in the house. Later, as the months passed by, we were allowed to have blue lights in the house which could not be seen from the outside.

Also, we had to have air-raid shelters built in the yard. My neighbor's son helped me dig the "L"-shaped shelter. We lined it with cardboard and stored canned goods and water in it. The top of the shelter was covered with tin and dirt. Whenever the sirens blew, we had to go in the shelter and stay there until the all clear siren was sounded.

Our lives were drastically changed because of the war. At that time I was a senior in high school. After the attack, all of the schools were closed.

We seniors didn't have to continue school when they reopened. We were still given our diplomas as long as we were working for the army.

Calls went out for workers. All available students went to the hospital where we were hired—no experience necessary.

I was hired at the ammunition depot in Wheeler Field where my job was to load bullets and tracers into ammunition belts. Later I was hired by the army as a secretary at an office which was stationed at Punahou School in Honolulu. I was later transferred to Schofield Barracks. While there, we were issued gas masks and given shots for all sorts of diseases.

Life changed for everybody during the war. Many enterprising individuals made fortunes by operating lunch wagons and selling food around the working areas because there were so many soldiers around.

All of the language schools (Japanese and Chinese) were closed during the war. As the years passed by, the schools were allowed to reopen.

Lifestyles changed from the war. Many of my friends married GIs. That was the beginning of interracial marriages in the islands. Up until then, the races rarely mixed in marriage.

When we were growing up, we felt that we were a lower class from whites (called *haole*) from the mainland USA. We hardly mingled with them socially. Nowadays, with all of the intermarriages, everybody seems to be on the same level.

THEODORE HO

On the morning of December 7, 1941, my two older brothers and I were in Sunday school class at the Salvation Army Mission. I was nine going on ten-years-old at that time. It was a beautiful Sunday morning—bright blue skies and hardly any clouds.

At 8:00 a.m., we started to hear explosions in the distance. The Salvation Army staff members came to the classroom and told the teachers that Pearl Harbor Navy Base was being attacked by Japanese airplanes. Pearl Harbor is about five to seven miles from Honolulu. We were told to rush home (we lived about a half-mile away). On the way home, we could see the clouds of black smoke from the direction of Pearl Harbor.

We stood in the lane in front of our house and watched the antiaircraft shells explode in the sky trying to down Japanese planes. We could see the rising sun insignia on their wing tips. Also, we watched in fascination as several Army Air Force P-40 Warhawk airplanes engaged several Japanese Zeros in dogfights. For some reason I was not frightened, just fascinated by what was happening.

The Japanese fighter and bomber aircraft did not strafe or bomb the city of Honolulu. Their primary target was the United States' Pacific Fleet at Pearl Harbor. They also attacked Hickam Army Air Field (next to Pearl

Harbor), Schofield Barracks (army base), Wheeler Army Air Field (next to Schofield Barracks), and Kaneohe Navy-Marine Air Station (on the other side of the island).

There were several explosions on the outskirts of the city. However, they were not from Japanese bombs but from antiaircraft shells that did not explode in the air and fell back to earth.

We fully expected an invasion force to follow that attack to take over the island. Fortunately, none followed. We listened to the radio (no television then) all day for reports and instructions. There were all kinds of reports by hysterical people saying that Japanese were landing near the reservoir and poisoning the water supply, small landing parties from submarines landing on remote beaches, etc.

The reality of war sank in as the sun set. There was to be no light—a complete blackout was to be maintained. The next day we listened to the radio as President Franklin D. Roosevelt addressed a joint session of Congress. He asked for a declaration of war against Japan and Germany. Congress overwhelmingly approved his request. During that day, we helped our parents rig sheets and curtains over all the windows and exit doors, and bought flashlights and batteries.

Several days later, FBI agents and army personnel came to the neighborhood and rounded up Japanese aliens as well as Japanese Americans. They also did this on the West Coast of the United States. Many government and military leaders believed that these Japanese citizens were still loyal to the emperor of Japan and would commit acts of espionage and sabotage. They were all moved to "relocation camps" in Utah, Nevada, and New Mexico. History proved that there was not one single act of espionage or sabotage committed by these loyal Americans.

My mom went to work at Pearl Harbor. Dad followed and worked as a machinist. He always had interesting stories to tell us about the crippled and bombed ships and aircraft that somehow made it back to Pearl Harbor for repairs and supplies—especially after the Battles of Coral Sea and Midway. These two naval battles were turning points of the war. The Japanese Imperial Navy was wiped out.

What a joyous day it was in August 1945 when Japan surrendered!

REVEREND DAN KONG

We lived right outside of Schofield Barracks in Wahiawa, just a half mile from Wheeler Field. When the Japanese attacked on the morning of the 7th, our house, like most of the homes back then, were just frame buildings. They began to shake and the windows were rattling, which woke us up.

I was twelve-years-old at the time. My brother and I shared a bedroom.

We looked out the window and saw planes flying very low. By the time the planes hit Wheeler, there was no opposition. There was very little return fire, so the pilots were able to fly with their cockpit canopies open. They could look right down on Wheeler and strafe their targets.

We ran out of the house with our pajamas on because we saw all of the smoke bellowing from Wheeler Air Force Base. Thirteen miles down the road was Hickam Field and Pearl Harbor.

Wahiawa is on a higher plateau, so I climbed up an avocado tree for a better view. Within a few minutes, my brother came running out and said, "Hey, let's go watch the fireworks!" Of course, you have to understand, we had no idea we were under attack. We just thought, "Wow, spectacular maneuvers."

My brother, who was sixteen, had just gotten his license. So we ran into the house, got into our street clothing, and drove right on to the air field. We did that regularly because my father was a cashier at the commissary of Schofield Barracks.

We could see all of these planes coming without any opposition, strafing and bombing. Every time we saw them drop something, we didn't know what it was. The ground shook and orange and red flames shot high into the sky.

A few minutes later, my brother said, "Hey, we better go home." We didn't have a radio in our car back then. We got home and turned on the old Philco radio and heard this commentator, Webley Edwards say, "This is the real McCoy. The Japanese forces of the Imperial Navy are attacking the island. Take cover!" From that moment on, it was no fun for us. It was scary because now we were under attack. Before it was just "tremendous maneuvers." We didn't know where we would take cover.

We turned on our shortwave radio and heard all sorts of rumors. There was also a lot of commotion going on outside, so we ran out just in time to see two P-40s up in the sky engaged in a dogfight with several Japanese planes. The P-40s came from an emergency landing field about five miles down the road. Most of the rest of the U.S. planes were destroyed because they were bunched up in clusters providing easy targets for the Japanese bombers.

A lieutenant by the name of Wells or Welsh and another man got airborne and were engaged in a fight. It was so traumatic for all of us. I believe one of our pilots shot down two Japanese planes, so he was a hero at that time.

The night after that, we were so frightened because we could hear the droning of planes and didn't know if the Japanese were coming back or not.

The more we thought about it, how the Japanese really caught us off guard, with most of the U.S.'s ammunition having been stored away, the Japanese planes could have landed and, perhaps, taken the island. We were really caught flat-footed.

Immediately following the attack, block wardens were selected. My dad was chosen. We were all issued gas masks.

Weeks or months later, we'd go by Pearl Harbor and say, "Wow, look at that, ninety-four ships in the harbor." The next day, they would all be gone and we'd say, "Oh, something's going to happen." Sure enough, two-and-a-half three weeks down the road Guadalcanal took place.

Later, I became a newsboy to the troops quartered at Schofield Barracks. People like Bob Hope and Joe DiMaggio came and I got to know some of these people. It was such a thrilling experience.

It is all so vivid in my mind—just like it happened yesterday. It was all so real to us. When we look back and reflect on it, we think, "Oh, by God's grace that we're still here."

ROSE WONG

I was a teenager at that time and lived right in the center of town. We heard the news on the radio and went out and looked up in the sky and here were all of these Japanese planes. We were just kids so we thought it was fun watching those planes fly back and forth over the house. We didn't know that we could've been killed.

In fact, one plane flew over the house and dropped a bomb which landed about a hundred yards or so away. The way the bomb felt, I thought the house had been hit. The entire house shook. There was a group of teenaged boys who were on their way to the gym on that Sunday morning. They were all killed by that blast. Upon impact, the flesh and body parts just flew and hung up in one of our trees.

My uncle was out in the road and came running into the house and told us not to go outside. He didn't want us to see what happened. That's when we looked out the window and saw the flesh in the trees. It was still burning.

After the attack, they imposed martial law. We had to go to dances in the daytime rather than night. We had to black out our windows with this thick black paper. We also had to have an air raid shelter so my uncle had to dig one which was real deep. He made it real nice. It had boards all around it and we would play in it at night. It had lights and we had a lot of fun in there.

ITSUKO NISHIKAWA

I was stunned to hear the news of the attack over the radio. It was around 7 or 8 a.m. Hawaii time, and we were just waking up.

We were about fifteen miles from Pearl Harbor and could feel a little bit of the actual bombing. We were scared and didn't know what was going to happen next. Our home was near a U.S. army base, Schofield Barracks. We were afraid the Japanese were going to come back and bomb the barracks and us too.

What I remember most were the aftereffects, mainly the blackouts. We couldn't turn on our lights without first blacking out our windows with something like tar paper. You weren't even allowed to have the smallest amount of light showing. Neighborhood block leaders would check it out and cite violators. Every now and then we would turn off all of the lights so we could open the doors and windows and air out the house.

It was particularly tough for my mother and father who were born in Japan and not naturalized. They had very little to say about the situation. For myself, my brothers, and my sisters, we had great loyalty towards the United States because we were all born here. We had little contact with Japan. Still, we felt sorry for our parents. They couldn't say anything. They were divided.

As Japanese Americans, I feel we were more fortunate than those on the mainland. We were so Americanized and accepted over here, so we weren't interned like many of those in the States. Japanese Americans were so much in the majority over here that they couldn't possibly intern all of us. The economy would have collapsed.

I also remembered the 100th Battalion and the 442nd Combat Team being organized and staffed by Japanese Americans intent on proving their loyalty to the United States. At first, most Japanese Americans weren't drafted into the service. These men volunteered and fought bravely over in Europe and suffered tremendous losses. My brother was with the infamous 442nd, the nation's only all Japanese American regimental combat team.

RUTH MATSUDA

I was living on Diamond Head in an architect's home in December 1941. I used to take care of the house. On the morning of the 7th, I was on my way to Wahiawa to dedicate the building site of the Wahiawa Baptist Church. When I was on Nimitz Highway, I saw a bomb falling on a ship parked in Pearl Harbor. I thought, "Now what is going on?" I was in a taxi, and on the way we were stopped by the authorities once. I didn't realize why. We told them of our destination and were allowed to pass.

I didn't know that Pearl Harbor had been attacked until I reached my parent's home in Wahiawa and my family told me how much they were worried about me. That's how I learned we were at war with Japan.

My family owned a trucking business and the authorities ordered them to go out and collect the bodies that had been shot and then fell in the pineapple fields. As a result, our trucks were allowed to be on the road so I was able to get back to Diamond Head.

The architect had a very large mansion with quite a bit of room, so he was the host to several officers in the military, as well as an American attaché to Japan. I would cook for all of them and they were pleased with my effort. I was able to talk to all of them because, even though I was of Japanese descent, I was an American citizen.

Shortly after the attack, the FBI came to my parent's house in Wahiawa. My father had just undergone cancer surgery and was very weak. They tried to pick him up and take him in. He explained his situation to them saying that he was just too weak to travel. They understood and let him be. That made us very grateful.

I had two brothers who served in the 442nd. One went to Europe to fight and ended up losing a leg in battle. Even though he came home on only one leg, my mother, who had been praying for his safety, was very happy to see him. He also returned with a bride, the sister of a Japanese American soldier he met while being hospitalized in Denver. That also made my mother very happy.

JUNE YOSHIDA

We were on the island of Kauai. The village where we lived was a sugar plantation, and our neighbors were predominantly Japanese. The news spread fast amongst the residences.

As a child, I remember the blackouts. We were put on a curfew. We weren't allowed to use regular lights in our homes at night. We had these light bulbs, the ones hanging from the ceiling, painted all black except for a small circle on the bottom. That allowed us just enough light to get around the house.

I also remember us having air-raid practices. They distributed gas masks to everybody. I remember these details because it was a very scary experience.

CHARLES KOBAYASHI

On that morning, I was at home having breakfast. We didn't hear the planes. We were in Kauai and the bombing was in Oahu. When we heard the news, we stopped eating and put our ears to the radio. Of course, we were all surprised to hear that the Japanese had bombed Pearl Harbor and could hardly believe it. But, as the news kept coming in, we realized that the United States was at war with Japan. We were all shocked. We were all praying that the war would end quickly.

When all of the neighbors talked, we realized that a great hardship was ahead for all of us. We thought that if the war goes on, we civilians would end up getting involved in it.

LOUIS OLSON

It seems like yesterday when my shipmates and I heard the news on the ship's radio. I was on the heavy cruiser USS *Northampton*, and we were escorting aircraft carriers and other miscellaneous ships in our Pacific Fleet back to Pearl Harbor. We had just delivered fighter planes to Wake Island and were within one day of Pearl when a line from a destroyer accidentally dropped into the sea and wrapped around one of our screws. It took the divers all day to unravel the mess, and meanwhile the entire fleet waited until our ship was underway again. So on December 8, we finally arrived at Pearl and saw what was left of battleship row. Many of the ships were still burning, badly damaged, or sunk. We thanked God the accident happened when it did or the Pacific Fleet would have been totally lost. From then on, we were on the offensive until our ship was sunk at Guadalcanal.

2
IMPRESSIONABLE YOUTH

There are more than a few difference between the young people of today and those growing up during the Depression years of the 1930s and 1940s. Compared with the present day, children growing up during the Depression did not have much in the way of material goods, but one thing they could count on was the dependability of the times. The movies on Saturday afternoon rarely cost more than ten cents, baseball's Yankees usually won, mom always saved the best meal of the week for Sunday dinner, and Roosevelt was always president.

The uniform peace of American life came to an abrupt halt on December 7, 1941. The news was especially troublesome to young people. While many could not grasp the concept of war, some children were excited about the prospect of the impending conflict. To their way of thinking, war was where the enemy was killed and you won. Others believed that their brothers and/or fathers would die for no other reason that a war was in progress and their relatives were in the armed forces. Still others believed, and with just cause, that a war could eventually spill over into the United States, into their towns, or even into their own homes.

In 1941, there were approximately 22 million young people in the range of five to fourteen years of age.[1] Between one-half to one-third of them could be classified as living in a rural setting.[2] One-third of all households in the United States still used wood or coal to cook or heat their homes.[3] Television was still several years from being a practical medium, so children of that time had to be a bit more creative when it came to entertaining themselves. One of the great pastimes was sitting in the living room "watching" the radio and imagining the wondrous scenes the actor was performing. Those same children soon found that the radio could also bring images of an unpleasant reality into their tranquil lives as well.

LOREN ROBINSON

That day, December 7, 1941, is still vivid in my mind, as it is with many of my generation. I lived in a small, North Idaho town called Priest River—a logging town of maybe 900 people. The nearest town of any size was Spokane, some sixty miles to the southwest. The Depression was just about over, and most of the men were back to work.

I was a freshman in school and on the basketball team. With a little over a hundred students, any boy who turned out made the team. That was lucky for me. On Saturday night, December 6, we traveled downriver to play Cusick, Washington, a school about our size. We felt good about the win, but nearly froze on the bus ride back home. The heater in the 1939 school bus didn't reach the rear.

The weather was clear on Sunday morning complete with brisk air and scattered clouds. With the sun shining down upon us, and not more than a foot of snow on the ground, the temperature hovered around fifty degrees. Dad roused me out of bed at 7 a.m., saying that grandfather needed help fixing a fence on his dairy farm.

My grandfather had a neighbor, a Spanish-American War veteran, by the name of Jess Miller. Mr. Miller didn't talk much, and I never saw him move fast. As my dad, grandfather, and I were working on the fence, Mr. Miller came barging out of his back door and charged across his hay field to the fence. I never saw him run so fast, even in the snow. He was out of breath and his face was flushed when he reached us.

He had been listening to the radio and told us about the attack. I had never heard of Pearl Harbor, and when dad and I got home, we looked it up on our world globe.

My older brother, a sophomore, and I sat with our folks the rest of the day listening to the radio. They were silent most of the time, and seemed to stare at my brother and me. Their solemn look told me they were quite concerned. My brother and I took it in stride. We never thought we would soon find ourselves in the South Pacific.

We were aware of the war in Europe—it was on the radio and in the papers everyday. Edward R. Murrow kept us posted on the bombing of London, and H. V. Kaltenborn always started his broadcast with, "There's bad news from Europe tonight."

At school, on Monday, Pearl Harbor was the topic of conversation. Everybody in town had sat by their radios on Sunday. I don't think the impact hit us kids as it did our parents. Seniors were probably more concerned than us freshmen.

When I was seventeen, I finished school and volunteered for the navy rather than waiting to be drafted.

BILL WOLL

I was ten-and-a-half-years-old on December 7, 1941. We heard the news of the bombing on the radio after my parents returned home from church. We lived in New York City at the time. We stayed glued to the radio for most of the afternoon. Later on in the day, a newsboy shouting, "Extra, Extra, news of the bombing!" came through our neighborhood, and most families ran out to purchase a copy of the newspaper.

Since my father was older, we knew he wouldn't have to go to war. He had served briefly in World War I and received a medical discharge. My mother became an air-raid warden, and I served as an air-raid messenger. We had armbands with lightning bolts on them and we could be outside during air-raid drills, which was a big deal.

In school, we had to wear plastic identification necklaces and get under our desks during air-raid drills.

The anti-Japanese and anti-Axis propaganda was intense and continuous. The media never let us forget who the enemy was! Children kept scrapbooks, and the war occupied four years of our lives. The war was front-page news every day, unlike the Korean War in which I participated. Then, weeks went by without a bulletin from that war zone.

V-E and V-J days were cause for wild celebration, and returning GIs were given parades and feted over and over again. Once again, a big difference from our treatment after the Korean War.

I was in high school from 1945 through 1949. Peace!!! We were all proud that our country was victorious.

VERDIE RICKERSON

On Sunday morning during church services, our pastor, H. O. Brunkau, announced the attack on Pearl Harbor. We didn't even have a radio so we had no way of knowing of this news until we got to church.

I lived in Elkhart, Kansas. I don't think I really realized the impact it had on me until I got home. Many in the congregation did display emotional trauma. When I got home, my two brothers, Troy and Tandy Hart, were already making plans to enlist in the armed forces. That was when I realized the horror of the attack. My mother was with me at church and was quite concerned, but really became upset when she found out that her two sons were planning to "go to war." Our father was a World War I vet, so she knew the impact of war and army life.

My dad said the boys should go to war if that's what they wanted. I wasn't sure if that was his true feeling or not.

I was a senior in high school and was scared to death. My older brother, Troy, enlisted and eventually went to France. Tandy did not pass the physical because he had one crossed eye. He was devastated. He was classified as 4-F, which later became a stigma to all young men who did not pass the physical. It was sad, but my mother and I felt relief that both of the boys didn't have to go. However, both of my parents spent many anxious years of anticipation as did many others.

Troy was fortunate enough to return home. Many of our friends did not return. The prayers and tears that were shed for all the boys were enough to last a lifetime.

It was a thought that after I graduated from high school I would join the army to be a nurse. Of course my folks were against it. The civilian hospitals were matching the stipend given by the military to attract student nurses. So to please my mother, I enrolled at the school of nursing at Scott and White Hospital in Temple, Texas. I was still tempted to go to the government hospital because the big McCloskey General Hospital was also in Temple, but I didn't. When I finished school, the war was over so I went back to Kansas to work in civilian hospitals.

Homer Rickerson, my husband, retired from the service after twenty-eight years. He was interesting to listen to when he and my brother Troy would get together and talk about World War II. They were both very military all of the way.

I retired from my nursing career after forty years—thirty-eight at the same hospital in Garden City, Kansas.

ROSE MITCHELL

I was sixteen-years-old and in Ebensburg, Pennsylvania, in a restaurant called Three Little Pigs. When the news came over the radio, the owner of the restaurant went into a rage. She grabbed a pink plastic pig off the shelf, and since it was made in Japan, literally squashed that pig between her hands. Everyone was telling everyone else and they too were furious.

I had two older brothers who were near draft age, and my family wondered how soon they would have to leave for the army.

The one thing I remember was how homes had a small flag in their windows telling how many people in their household were in the service. Each star represented a soldier from that house.

JAMES ERICKSON

On December 7, 1941, my cousin and I went to a matinee at the Rhodes Theater at 79th and Rhodes Ave. on the south side of Chicago. Upon our return around 6 p.m., my uncle advised us that the "Japs" had attacked our naval base at a place called Pearl Harbor, and we were at war. The available facts involving the fleet damage were sketchy.

Later that evening there was a report that we had sunk a Japanese sub. I was sure, in my ten-and-a-half-year-old mind, that the war would soon be over as a result of this particular sub sinking and that the Japanese military would be begging for mercy.

DOLLIE CHILDS

I was in elementary school when I heard the news. I lived in the small town of Clanton, Alabama, and the teachers took our class time to show us maps of where the island of Hawaii was and what had happened. School was let out early that day because everyone was so upset. Those whose parents could come and pick them up were allowed to use the office phone to call them. An announcement was made that there would be no bus service the next week as school busses were needed to take volunteers and new recruits to Montgomery.

Anyone who wanted to volunteer had to give their name at the post office by Saturday. They knew if they didn't volunteer, they would have to fill out draft cards and be scheduled for a physical. Saturday morning, the busses were loaded in front of the movie house. The high school band played, and everyone was waving a flag and crying. We had no television, so every night our movie house was packed, no matter what was playing, because war news was shown before the movie.

Businesses were in need of employees to replace those who went into the service. Those left behind were wives and mothers. All were willing to do their share.

There was also a great shortage of gasoline, tires, and sugar. They issued books with stamps, so everyone had the same opportunity to buy what was available. Everyone had to have the stamps to get what they needed. People shared their transportation and stamps for purchasing gas and tires.

I helped my grandfather, who had a small grocery store, after school and on Saturdays. I would have to collect toothpaste tubes and the aluminum from gum wrappers and put them into a cigar box. I would give them to my grandfather when the box was full. Everyone had to cut back as times were hard.

I was given a small allowance, and my parents encouraged me to go every week to the post office to buy savings bonds stamps. When the booklet was filled, they would exchange the full book for a savings bond in my name.

Life magazine was popular in the homes, for there were write-ups with pictures that let us know what was going on. There were also announcements on the radio, for anyone that had old cars or anything metal, to contact them and donate it because it was needed to make tanks and guns.

The town was prepared for air raids, should an attack occur. We were put on a civil alert. To the best of our abilities, we were ready for whatever might happen. We listened for the warning siren. Everyone cleared the exits safely. All the homes observed lights out. Rather than being in total darkness, shades were used in most homes. Anyone not doing as they were told was given a fine. Cars were instructed to pull off the road, cut out the lights, and remove themselves to a safer place, whenever possible, during the drills. Radios were on an instruction program until the "all clear" siren was given. We trusted that we were in good hands. Our country cared and, with God's help, we were going to make it.

My mother grieved over the loss of her youngest brother, Davis McAlister. He was on a secret mission and his plane was shot down. They never found the plane. Almost every family shared the loss of a loved one in this war.

After my father's death, my mother asked me to find out more of what had happened to her brother. So, we traveled to Hawaii and toured the grave sites of so many Americans. When we took the boat trip out to the *Arizona* memorial my mother cried when she saw the names of all who lay entombed on that ship.

We went to the Schofield Barracks where her brother stayed whenever he was at that island. On the back of a monument paying tribute to those killed in the islands, mom found Wake and Midway Island on the painted map. She pointed to where she felt her brother's plane must have been hit. Ten years after my mother passed away, a book titled *The History Of Navy Patrol Bombing Squadron 118* (1992) was released with all the answers to what happened to her brother.

Our hearts were touched with the loss of our loved ones and the families of those who were killed in Hawaii. Waikiki is a living memorial to this event. They say, on that day, flowers are dropped from helicopters to float on the waters near the big clock near Pearl Harbor. I don't think anyone will ever forget that day and I pray we will never have to experience anything like that again.

Richard Hofmann

My parents, Dorothy and Harry Hofmann, had a cabin at Santa Cruz near the river when I was only five-years-old. We were up there, just waking up on an early Sunday morning, when some friends who had a cabin across the river called over to us and yelled, "The Japs are bombing Pearl Harbor!" My parents told them to "Go back to bed and sleep it off," figuring they were still drunk from a Saturday night party.

They said, "If you don't believe me, go turn on the radio!" This we did and found out the bad news. My father went back home to the Bay Area leaving my mother and me to stay up in the cabin. He didn't know if the Japanese were going to attack the Bay Area or not, and was getting his shotgun to fight them off if they invaded.

A week later, he came back up to Santa Cruz and got me and my mother to take us back home after the emergency was over.

Bud Overn

I clearly remember December 7, 1941. Dad had taken us for a ride down the California coast that morning. When we stopped at Oceanside for a break, we heard the news: "Japs bomb Pearl Harbor!" I remember the excitement of the newsboys shouting their headlines, and radios blaring the latest news reports: "War In The Pacific!" I remember a feeling of déjà vu—a somewhat smug feeling that I knew this was going to happen. I'd read about it for years in *Flying Aces* Magazine.

At first I awed and impressed with the prognostications of those 1930s pulp writers in *Flying Aces*. Later, however, I realized that Japan's ambitions with regard to the Pacific were well known, so it wouldn't have been too difficult for an aware, informed writer to weave this information into a story.

A writer named Arch Whitehouse wrote about a character named Buzz Benson. Benson, and many other pulp figures in *Flying Aces*, continued to point up the dangers of Japanese peril in the Pacific. In fact, the villains were so consistently portrayed as Japanese that some California *nisei* (second generation Japanese Americans) wrote to complain. *Flying Aces* apologized somewhat.

Some stories in *Flying Aces* were so prophetic of the possibility of war in the Pacific, including the times and places, that one has to wonder if the Japanese military used *Flying Aces* for their battle plan.

So war did come to the Pacific just as those writers had predicted. Even so, the next day at school was spent with a strange feeling of mixed emotions. Our Japanese schoolmates, whom we so admired for their outstanding ability in gym, art, math, etc., seemed very ashamed and sad. We sat in numbed silence as FDR made his "Day of Infamy" speech via the little radio brought into class. One Japanese girl broke down sobbing and ran from the room. I never saw her again. It was a terrible experience. We were filled with conflicting emotions when our Japanese American friends were rounded up and shipped off to "relocation centers." Sherman was right, "War is hell!"

When someone yells "Fire!" in a theater, people panic and do irrational things. Someone yelled, "Pearl's on fire and California is next!" So . . . we panicked, in hindsight, and did things that some now see as irrational. But after all, hadn't we been reading stories for years of their treacherous plans and, "How come they went to Japanese schools after regular school?" (I didn't go to a Norwegian school). "Were they studying their culture or learning how to be spies?" One is prone to paranoid ideas when there are war clouds on the horizon.

I tried to continue my life, trying not to think about the fact that I would be drafted out of high school and probably be involved in the invasion on the mainland of Japan (the bomb changed all that).

On Friday evening, March 10, 1933, I was playing in the alley between our house and Benton Way, when all of the windows started to shake. After that devastating Long Beach earthquake, we had earthquake drills in school—that is, until December 7, 1941. Then it was air-raid drills.

On February 24, 1942, dad awakened me to see searchlights and anti-aircraft fire over Inglewood. To this day, I really don't know what happened that night. Rumors had it that the jittery crew was shooting at seagulls or, worse yet, one of our own planes! Personally, I was convinced that we were being invaded.

With that in mind, I had a plan. I was in class with Charles Hathaway. We envied him as he was being chauffeured to school while we were playing in the dirt. He may have been envying us. Once he invited me to his birthday party at their mansion. The three mansions on the estate had a 360 degree view of greater Los Angeles, Hollywood, Los Feliz, Glendale, and Edendale (also known as "movie hill" because of the Mack Sennett movie studio). In case of an attack, I would flee into the Garbutt/Hathaway estate and hide inside a large, hollow artificial boulder left over from the early movie industry. I guess I was more afraid of the enemy than spiders!

Joe Kral Sr.

On December 7, 1941, I was sitting on the floor in front of our radio, which had a small dial in the center for stations, when a man, the announcer, said that Pearl Harbor was being bombed. I, Joe Kral, from Youngstown, Ohio, was ten-years-old at the time. I believe it was late in the morning.

This was the old days when movies cost five cents on Saturdays and ten cents on Sundays. I still remember breaking Japanese dishes on the street in front of our house in anger.

My two brothers served in the military during World War II, John in the army who won a Silver Star for gallantry at Anzio, Italy, and Jerry who served with the Coast Guard.

I'm sixty-seven-years-old now. I served with the army as a ski trooper and with the navy. I saw forty countries, forty states, and three oceans between 1949 and 1970.

Nita Johnson

That Sunday, December 7, 1941, began as an exciting day for a fourteen-year-old girl who lived for roller skating (and boys too, of course). But that day, my mind was only on roller skating. This was the day I was to take my first proficiency test on roller skates.

I was excited, scared, and eager for this big day in my life as I donned my cute, short skating dress made by my mother just for that day. I then laced up my skates and started getting ready for the "Big Event." Several of my friends were rolling around too, nervous and giggling as teen girls do. Even though it was early on a Sunday morning, we were alive and ready for our big challenge.

The judges arrived and our anxiety heightened. Right at that point, an announcement came over the loud speaker: "Any military personnel report to the office immediately." There was only one man in the military at the rink that day. He was also waiting to take his proficiency test.

His name was Dwight and he rushed to the office and got the news of the attack on Pearl Harbor. He came out of the office, ashen faced, as we gathered around him and heard the awful news. He also requested to be tested first as he had to report for duty immediately.

We all said, "Yes, certainly, go ahead," which he did. He somehow passed the test and dashed out the door. We didn't see him again for the next four years, but he did survive to skate again.

The rest of us somehow got through our tests and passed, but the test medal didn't seem quite as bright with a war hanging over our heads. However, I must add, we were so young and full of optimism that we really didn't realize the awful years ahead of us. We just assumed the U.S.A. would quickly put an end to the whole thing and our lives would go on as usual.

Of course we had to revise that optimism as the months and years of war were with us through the rest of our teen years. Most of us lost a friend or relative to the war, and we lost our innocence as we realized our country was in danger.

We all pitched in to do whatever we could in the war effort. I celebrated my eighteenth birthday by giving my first contribution of blood on October 13, 1944. I later married a man who was wounded on October 13, 1944. I told him it was my blood which saved his life.

PAUL J. ZDANOWICZ

I was home at age fifteen, a sophomore at Portland, Maine, high school, and we heard on the radio that FDR, the president, would declare war the next day. The next day at school we were all sent to four or five large study halls where teachers had been asked to bring radios from home.

We heard FDR's statement that "a state of war exists between our government and the Empire of Japan." Immediately after the broadcast, many of the young men, especially the seniors and juniors, got up and started out of the room. The teacher asked where they were going. They responded as one, "To the nearest recruiting office to sign up."

WILLIAM GREGORY

When the attack on Pearl Harbor occurred, I was fourteen years of age and at home listening to the radio, My father, mother, four brothers, and an uncle were in our living room talking. Upon hearing the news, my uncle immediately left the house to join the U.S. Army.

We were living in the country and owned a small drive-in restaurant/gasoline station. My father was employed with the Johnstown, Pennsylvania, water company during the day and worked the restaurant/gasoline station in the evenings and weekends.

Our lives were impacted immediately. Gasoline became rationed, tires were not available, and most food items were also rationed. The country roads became deserted because of the gasoline and tire allotments. We had to close the business and move ten miles to the city. We were lucky because my father had a job with the water company.

The following May, at fifteen years of age, I became a volunteer member of the Army Air Force Aircraft Warning Service. We were attached to the Army Air Force 1st Fighter Command located at Mitchel Field in New York. I could identify all enemy aircraft, even at night, by viewing their silhouettes. I knew how many engines they had by listening to their sounds. After school, I worked at a tire recapping facility, capping tires from synthetic rubber. I also worked at a welding facility making some war materials.

When the war ended, I was in my third year of high school. After graduation, I enlisted in the U.S. Navy Reserve. I badly injured my leg in an accident and was medically discharged from the U.S. Navy Reserve. While waiting for my leg to heal, I studied electronics and later opened my own repair service.

BARBARA DIDION

The family had just returned from church and my father turned the radio on. At first we couldn't place Pearl Harbor, then my brother got out our atlas and we found it. It was still hard for us to make the connection because we lived in southern Florida.

The next day at school, we were all taken to the auditorium to listen to the president make a wonderful speech in Congress. Some time later I saw President Roosevelt in the newsreel at a theater delivering the same speech.

I remember quite well what, where, and how I learned that America had entered the war, especially so because my family and myself spoke our native German at home. The people in the small town we lived in were very malicious towards us! I will never forget nor forgive what happened to myself and family.

Actually, our family name was French. My father and grandfather came to the United States from France. This is one of the reasons it was so heartbreaking for my family to be called Nazis and Krauts, etc.

You have to realize how hard this was on our family. My ancestors on my mother's side had fought in the Revolution, Civil War, and my grandfather had fought in the Spanish-American War. My father had been a soldier in World War I. Then when war was declared with Japan, the persecution from the town's people really went into high gear.

ALICE J. REID

It was one of those usual Sunday mornings. A cool, pale gray sky arched over silent streets while the houses on our "flatland" block looked as closed as the Sunday shops. But there was activity behind those shut doors. Daddy was home, Sunday school loomed, and Mama was in the kitchen, clad in an after bath Kimono over her petticoat, scented with Yardley's "April Violets," preparing the beginnings of the Sunday dinner. It was a most usual morning.

My sister and I put on our neat, homemade muslin dresses, buckled our "dress up" dollar ninety-nine Mary Janes, and tied bright grosgrain ribbons around the ends of our black braids. I was thirteen and barely aware of things of great importance, and I was never alarmed by the newspaper headlines Daddy discussed with Mama.

We ambled home from church under a pale sun. Mama whipped up a yellow cake and we did our small chores. We trailed after our father around the yard for a while, pleasantly Sunday bored.

The house began to be filled with the mouthwatering aromas of baking chickens and simmering vegetables—all gotten out of our own yard. We were "poor" black folks but didn't know it until well-meaning people told us we were. We had the garden, along with the chickens and their eggs. My sister and I helped with the canning during the summer—like the squirrels, we stored for the winter. We learned to sew, quilt, and mend, and managed to stay well through work and Grandma's old remedies.

Daddy drew tiny wages from a railroad and Mama often did day work up in the Berkeley Hills where white people dwelt. Racism thrived in Berkeley, my hometown, but we blacks in the "flatlands" got by. We had nearby kinfolks and neighbors for comfort and arguments! But in a few hours, a great change would come which would have ramifications the world's still feeling today.

Two or three of us youngsters were sitting on the sunny steps with Mickey, our dog, who lived with us for fifteen wonderful years. Mr. Collins came running across the street and up our driveway. "They bombin' Pearl Harbor! Get your radio on!" he shouted. We just gawked. Then people came out, and up and down the block, exclaiming and looking up at the sky. Little groups gathered and broke out on the sidewalk calling to each other.

Pearl Harbor—most had heard the name. The Bay Area was Navy— you saw sailors here and there. There were sailors' shops in every city. Stewards' mates brought home beautiful little teapots.

"It's a war!" a man said to two others. I still remember the glint in his eye. War. What was a war for? Why were these grown-ups so excited?

Our two-piece "candlestick" phone rang and rang again. The radio was loud. Erroneous stories circulated and rumors were fast born. Some men, World War I veterans like my father, slid into their basements with a "bottle." Our neighbor, Mr. Johns, was a chief steward stationed at tiny Goat Island, and I think he had a field day. He was already in the service, you see. He retired from duty years later.

I do recall some of the mothers. Mrs. Martin went up to the nearby Lorin Theater and got her kids. Other mothers spoke of the bombing. One or two estimated the ages of sons, nephews, and distant cousins. Their glances were already anxious.

My mother called us in and rather sternly told us to set the table. We were still going to eat our dinner. In those days, families ate together— off of tablecloths yet! Years later, I idly asked her why she was so cross that afternoon. She said that she wasn't angry, she just knew that things were going to change. Everything did.

GENE EIKLOR

I had just turned twelve a few weeks before December 7th. On that cold, sunny Sunday, my mother, brother, and I went by bus to my mother's cousin for our Christmas dinner. My mother had been raised by this particular cousin since age two. There was a sixteen-year age spread. She was more the aunt than the cousin.

The dinner was roast pork, mashed potatoes, gravy, and cauliflower. I don't remember the dessert. When we finished eating, my brother, cousin, and I were sitting in the dining room bay window seat playing a game.

My cousin had a radio station on that was playing the "Hit Parade" songs of the week. The show was interrupted to announce that Pearl Harbor had been attacked by the Japanese. My cousin, who was a few years older, went out to tell her mother and my mom. To this day I can hear the words of my mother's cousin. "That G— D— Roosevelt!" I don't remember much more of what she said.

When we went to get on the early Greyhound bus to go home, I remember it was windy with freezing rain.

BILL SHOTWELL

Pearl Harbor occurred the day after my sixth birthday. I don't recall my reaction at hearing the news that day, nor that of my classmates, but the days that followed were filled with small groups of people passing on any news they may have heard on the radio.

The war in Europe had been going on for some time, and we all had been following the maps and news accounts in the newspapers and on the radio. But, living in a small town in northeastern Pennsylvania, we didn't feel affected as yet. The only thing our town had that was of any significant value was the repair yards for the Erie Railroad.

My father worked for the railroad and had been given both a draft deferment and additional ration coupons for gas so that he could get out to work on the trains that needed his expertise. He was the superintendent of car heating and lighting for the Erie.

My family and I gathered around the radio the day the President announced the bombing attack on Pearl Harbor and our entry into World War II. It was all very exciting to a six-year-old, and the days that followed were filled with activities related to the war effort. We collected scrap metal, rubber, and cooking fat and turned them in each Saturday at our school. At the time I wasn't sure why we were doing this, but it was what we had been asked to do, so we did it. For this we were given small red (really pink), white, and blue ribbons that we wore proudly.

Eventually, men from the town began to enlist and go off to war while their parents hung small flags in their windows proudly proclaiming that they had a son in the army. I don't remember our town losing any sons in the war, but I'm sure a six-year-old would not have been told of the fact if it had occurred. We followed the maps in the paper every evening. The paper didn't carry any pictures. We listened to the radio, mainly WOR in New York, as the war progressed. I remember that a house, two blocks away, caught fire during an air raid drill, and I was convinced that it had been bombed.

The war was won in the Pacific when I was ten-years-old. By this time, my father had taken a job that required that we move to California. It was interesting to me to see that people who had lived there throughout the war were still quite concerned about the Japanese menace from the west (across the ocean).

We lived near the Alameda Naval Air Station and it was wonderful seeing all of those military planes flying around the Bay Area. It was very heady stuff for a ten-year-old. I knew every plane type and every ship that came into port, very heady stuff.

Over the years I've become convinced that being exposed to the war at such an early age colored my thinking on many subjects ever since.

TOM STEPWITH

In 1941, I was still in high school. As I recall, it was a relatively warm day in Cleveland on the 7th. At a quarter after two, I was just leaving church. As I walked home with a friend of mine, nothing was said about the attack. When I got home, the radio was on. It was about twenty-five after 2 p.m. when I heard them mention that there was an attack on Pearl Harbor.

A lot of people didn't know where Pearl Harbor was, but I did. I was a bit of a geography nut as a kid. I also collected stamps from around the world, so I knew where Pearl Harbor was. It was still quite a surprise and a shock.

During the war, I worked for Union Carbide. I earned enough money to put myself through Ohio State University where I received my degree in landscape architecture. I hold several landscape design patents in both Japan and the United States highlighting many of the key Pacific sites pertaining to the war.

FLORA MIZRAHIE

When the Japanese attacked Pearl Harbor, I was living in Calcutta, India. I was seventeen-years-old at the time and in my last year of school. I do not remember what time of day it was, but to us, being so far away, it did not mean much at the time. We knew that there was a war going on. The attack occurred two days before my birthday.

The day of the attack was a beautiful Indian winter's day. We read the news in the prestigious Calcutta newspaper—*The Statesman*.

I think the news impacted my father most of all. He was an importer/exporter at that time, importing goods from Germany and Japan and exporting goods to Burma. He had a flourishing business, and the shop in Rangoon, Burma, was run by his two brothers. He did all of the ordering of the goods from Calcutta and sent them by ship to Rangoon.

My father knew immediately that his business was in trouble. In a few months we heard that the Japanese had invaded Burma and taken over all the businesses, etc. His brothers contacted him and he told them that they would have to leave Burma and move to Calcutta.

They packed what few belongings they were able to carry, and because they were not able to travel by sea, started their trek towards Calcutta by road and train. It took them between six weeks and two months to arrive in Calcutta.

Having lost his business, my father had to find other means of supporting his family. He turned to making cheese and wine.

In the few months after the Japanese took over Burma, the British knew that the next invasion would be in India. At that time, the British were still in possession of India. They implemented the ARP (Air Raid Precaution) Program. This necessitated turning on the lights as little as possible after dark, pulling down the shades in our homes, and avoiding lighting candles or carrying flashlights.

And then the bombing started. The first area the Japanese bombed was the docks. We were asked to avoid that area unless we were working there. The newspapers gave accounts of the air raids and about the British Spitfires and their skirmishes with the Japanese planes. I remember very well one particular headline in the newspaper: "Three Enemy Planes Shot Down in Four Minutes" and the name of the pilot, Sgt. Pring, who had shot them down.

By the year 1944, and after gaining a lot of experience as a secretary, I landed a secretarial job in the baggage department of the American Army headquarters in Calcutta. It was called the CBI (China-Burma-India) theater of operations. The salary I made was a great help in feeding our family. There was some rationing like with sugar, etc., but with fruits and vegetables, they were very cheap. We had no food worries.

In 1946, if I remember well, the American military left Calcutta, but a division called AGRS (American Graves Registration Service) continued to operate until some time in 1948. I continued to work in this department until they left.

Veronica McKnight

My parents were Russian and German, having fled Russia during the Revolution in the early 1920s. During the Revolution in Russia, dad's parents were stripped of all of their land, so they emigrated to China, Korea, and eventually to Japan. When they fled Russia, they became stateless, and because of their origin in Germany, they decided to take out German papers, not knowing that Hitler would become Germany's leader.

We were living in Tokyo, Japan, when the war clouds became thick in 1940 and 1941. I was attending an American school with an enrollment of many international students. We were making plans to immigrate to the United States. Unfortunately, many Americans left the Orient in 1941 on the advice of the State Department, fearing that war would break out. The lack of paying students forced the closure of the school. I had no option but to be enrolled in a German school that fall.

War rumors persisted, and on December 7, 1941, much to our horror, we heard over the Japanese radio that Pearl Harbor had been bombed. My dad had been employed by 20th Century Fox films as a sales manager, importing their movies for showing in Japanese theaters. The company closed its doors, and he was out of a job.

My mother was a housewife, and I was fourteen-years-old. We had no income whatsoever. Because we were considered "friendly" nationals (with German papers), the Japanese secret police, or *Kempetai*, came to our home that day and told us we would not be repatriated or imprisoned. However, we were always regarded with suspicion by the Japanese since the general population had no way of knowing what nationality we were. The *Kempetai* paid us numerous, unannounced visits ostensibly to chat to see how we were getting along. Actually, they were there to snoop around to see if we used a shortwave radio to get news from other sources.

Eventually, Dolittle's incendiary raids on Tokyo forced the Japanese government to resettle all foreigners, including French, Italian, German, Russian, and others not involved in Japan's war against the United States, into mountainous areas.

We endured many hardships, food and housing wise, but were fortunate to have survived those dreadful years. Eventually, during the U.S. occupation of Japan in 1945, I met the man who would become my husband, married him, and left for the United States in 1948. My parents followed a few years later. I am extremely grateful to be a U.S. citizen and to be living in this country.

Scott Leesberg

I was only twelve-years-old and returning with my mother and father from a visit to my relatives in Fostoria, Ohio. They decided to stop at a friend's house in Oberlin, Ohio. The friend was a ham operator and was in contact with an operator in Hawaii. The Hawaiian ham operator did not have a great deal of firsthand information, but he was relaying the facts that he did know about the attack on Pearl Harbor. After a brief period, the Hawaiian said that he had been notified that all transmissions from the Islands were to cease and we lost contact with him.

I had no real sense of where Hawaii was. I knew it was in the Pacific, and my parents gave me some sense of the location, but it was still very vague. I had traveled through the East with my parents and grandfather, but I had never been west of Ohio so I had no feeling for the vast distances involved. My parents were more able to comprehend the enormity of what we were hearing and conveyed the sense of it to me.

Even though we were still living in very tough economic times, I believe that most citizens of the United States were extremely sheltered from the realities of the world situation.

My mother and father were quite diligent in listening to the news broadcasts and reading the newspaper accounts of what was happening, so I picked up that habit. I had listened on the radio to Adolf Hitler's harangues, and while they were in a language I didn't understand, it was obvious that he was a real rouser. I remember seeing the newsreel pictures of the huge crowds listening and shouting, "Sieg Heild," and that gave a dimension to the things that I heard. I heard a great deal of criticism of Hitler and the Axis since we were staunch supporters of the Allies. There had been much bad news about how the war in Europe was going, and I think I knew that there were talks in Washington with the Japanese because it was in the newspapers. However, I know that my parents considered the attack even more treacherous because the Japanese diplomats were talking peace while the Japanese fleet was on the way to bomb Pearl Harbor.

Like everyone else, I found the staggering losses that followed Pearl Harbor to be unbelievable. There was really no good news. There were reports of heroism, but these were always in a losing cause. Colin Kelly diving his B-17 into a Japanese warship, the commander of the marine contingent on Wake Island who, when asked if there was anything he needed said, "Send us more Japs!", and MacArthur's escape from the Philippines, were examples of the good news that had to satisfy our desire to win the war.

Most of the news was really bad. The loss of most of the South Pacific countries, the threat to Australia, the sinking of the HMS *Hood*, the loss of Singapore, the Bataan "Death March," the fall of Corregidor, etc. It was hard to find any good news except at the movies.

In August 1945, I was going to travel by Greyhound bus to visit a friend who had moved to Orlando, Florida. As we were preparing to depart for the bus station, it was announced that the Japanese had surrendered. The trip through the downtown area was a memorable experience. It was like the pictures in the papers of Times Square. People were everywhere. Soldiers and sailors were kissing all of the girls and the girls were apparently responding with the enthusiasm of the moment.

We passed through Cincinnati after dark and the town was still jumping and celebrating. Since these were the times before superhighways, I remember traveling through little towns where they were firing off fireworks that night. All in all, it was a very impressive way to celebrate the end of the war.

REID TAUBE

I was twelve and with my parents in Columbus, Ohio, that weekend. We were house hunting as my dad had been transferred to Columbus from Cincinnati. Dad put us on the train to Cincy Sunday afternoon. After we settled into our seats and the train got under way, my mother noticed the other passengers were all chattering away with long, serious faces. She asked a gentleman what the commotion was about. He told us of the Japanese attack.

The Japanese military conquests and brutalities in the mid-1940s made them quite unpopular and feared. I recall playing with friends and we would sometimes switch from mock cowboy versus Indian battles to American soldiers versus "dirty Jap" mock battles.

Details of the Pearl Harbor attack were few and far between. All we could do was wonder what impact this all might have as we moved to a different city. We also worried that my dad, age thirty-seven, might get drafted if manpower needs became severe. He was the office manager for International Harvester. Since their main focus was farm equipment, which needed to feed the nation, he was put pretty far down on the draft call list.

BERT WETZEL

Sundays are usually devoted to church going, rest, and the pursuit of pleasurable things. However, one Sunday long ago, but stamped in the memories of those now in their senior years, came the shattering news.

December 7, 1941, stands out as a red-letter day on any American calendar as few others do. Suddenly and without warning, the sea and air forces of Japan struck our naval base at Pearl Harbor, Hawaii, raining death upon thousands of people and inflicting terrible property damage. Within an hour, much of the Pacific Fleet was either sunk or badly damaged. In one day, the United States would be at war—one that would change America forever.

My own recollections are that of a high school boy, who, like millions of others, was singing and humming popular ballads of the day such as "Chattanooga Choo Choo," "Elmer's Tune," and others. One of my Norfolk, Virginia classmates was a girl who would go on to become one of America's most popular vocalists, Keely Smith, or Dot Keely as she was known then.

This Sunday was a usual one at the Wetzel household. Mom was busy making one of her great Sunday dinners. Dad was in his shop working until noon as most florists did in those days.

It was around noon when the phone rang. Mom answered it. On the line was a Mrs. Leahy, one of my father's customers. We found Mrs. Leahy to be a charming lady, but there was an air of mystery to her. She claimed to be the daughter-in-law of Admiral Leahy, President Roosevelt's close advisor and envoy to Vichy, France. In the course of the conversation, she told mother that her son was on his way to Japan. This was before the news of Pearl Harbor had reached us. What a direction to be headed for, I thought. We never found out if he turned back, nor did we ever find out if Mrs. Leahy was actually the daughter-in-law of the admiral, for we never heard from her again.

After dinner, the folks were taking their usual Sunday afternoon naps and I was behind my drawing board penning my cartoon strip, Ace Burroughs. Suddenly, from the little radio on the windowsill, came the news about Pearl Harbor. I quickly awakened my folks and we all just stood there, stunned at the news.

Later in the afternoon we took a ride. The day was bleak, so symbolic of the terrible news that had reached us. Along Church Street, some Japanese businessmen were being rounded up by the police. Some were aliens.

As we headed for home, we came to a bus stop where two of my old friends from another side of town where we had lived were waiting for the bus home. They had just come from the movies and had not known about Pearl Harbor. They said, "Well, here we go," meaning into the armed forces and to war.

The next day, we all assembled in the school auditorium to hear President Roosevelt asking Congress to declare war on Japan. The popular fighting song of the day was "Let's Remember Pearl Harbor." And we damn sure did until we made the Japanese never forget it as well.

John C. Moore

I was nine-years-old, and on that particular Sunday morning we were on our way to my dad's sister's in his 1936 Ford. Now, my aunt lived thirty-six miles from us, and back then that was almost a half-day's drive.

The car was equipped with a radio, and we were listening to Gene Autry's "Melody Ranch" when the news of the attack on Pearl Harbor interrupted the program. It wasn't a big deal to me and my sister, as we probably didn't really understand the circumstances, but my parents went into shock at the news. However, we decided to continue the trip to my aunt's.

As luck would have it, we had a blowout. We went to a nearby service station to purchase a new tire, but as the news spread, the attendant wouldn't sell us a new tire. He did sell us an old used one, that was in worse shape than the one that blew out, but it got us to our aunt's and back. Trying to purchase fuel at that time was also difficult, as they only sold it in five-gallon increments.

My older brother enlisted in the navy the following week.

Lorrie Zernickow

I was a little girl at the time of Pearl Harbor, as I was born in 1937. I remember listening to the radio for all my favorite shows like *Captain Midnight, Jack Armstrong—The All-American Boy*, and others whose names I can't recall. The programs were interrupted to talk about the war, and

I can remember the president being on the radio. Even at that young age, I realized it must be important because the adults were all gathered around the radio and saying, "Shhhh," if I tried to ask a question.

My parents were divorced but my mom tried to explain what "war" and "bombings" were. But, it was like a fairy tale to me because it was happening somewhere else.

After Pearl Harbor, when my dad was sent to Hawaii while in the navy, I was only upset because he was very far away and I couldn't visit him like I did before. He sent me a silver bracelet with each of the Hawaiian Islands on it, and Oahu had a Pearl. I still have the bracelet but it is missing Oahu. It was my most precious possession even then.

Living with my German and Hungarian grandparents while my mom worked, I recall helping Granny mix the oleo with the little orange dot enclosed in the package so it would look like butter. I always went shopping with her, so ration stamps were very familiar to me.

Dinner conversation went right by me as it was mostly about Germany and the Japanese—things I understood very little about.

The effect on our lives seemed minimal to me, in that everything seemed to go on as it always had. I felt bad about the people across the ocean who were being bombed, but there was apparently nothing we could do about it.

P. BRIDEN

I was six-years-old at the time. I recall thinking the Statue of Liberty was in Pearl Harbor (I grew up on Long Island). Going to New Jersey to visit relatives, I prayed that our ferry boat wouldn't hit any of the buoys in the water since I thought they were mines.

The aftermath is still quite vivid in my mind. Things such as saving scrap metal, selling war bond stamps (as a Girl Scout), using rationing books for food are all memories.

I don't remember feeling deprived at all, but that is from the mind of a six-year-old. I do feel quite strongly that the next generation needs to know of our experiences. I guess it's true what they say, when one does not know history, one is doomed to repeat it.

JOANNE MILLER

I was only nine-years-old when Pearl Harbor occurred. I remember hearing it on the radio that my mother and father were listening to. I remember being a little frightened, thinking that airplanes would be flying over us and bombing us. My younger brother was seven at the time, and we talked about it at bedtime. I don't think we asked many questions, but we did listen to the grown-ups talk about war, and did hear President Roosevelt. We were very worried. My older half brothers were old enough to join the army and did. One of them joined the paratroopers. My father really worried about him, especially on D-Day. Of course we didn't know if he made it or not until much later. He was in the 101st Airborne.

My parents were air wardens in our farm community. We stayed in the house with our grandparents when they had to practice air-raid drills. This was really frightening to us as children because that meant that we could actually be bombed. We had to pull the shades and make sure no light showed outside. We also had the little rationing books for sugar, meat, and gas.

My mother worked at the OPA, which was a government agency that handled rationing. She had her picture in the paper when she issued rationing meat stamps to a Seeing Eye dog and his master. My grandmother had big pictures of several generals like Marshall, Patton, and MacArthur. She also hung the little flag with two stars in the window, signifying that we had two sons in the service of our country. My brother and I had some cutouts of all the war planes, that glowed in the dark, pasted to our bedroom ceiling so we could identify them. We wrote to my brothers on V-mail which was a special paper that was photographed and reduced to the size of a postage stamp. That was sent to an APO address, then enlarged enough to be read by the soldiers. This saved space on the ships and planes.

My oldest brother was stationed in Italy and never saw battle, but my next oldest brother was in D-Day, Holland, and several other battles. He was never injured. We were very proud of him.

By the time the war ended, I was in high school and had learned much more about the cause and effect of war. I hoped that there would never be any more war. I never could understand why problems could not be solved by other means. So many people have suffered so much because of man's inability to get along with others.

Richard A. Segal

On Sunday, December 7, 1941, I was nine-years-old and listening to Jack Benny on the radio in my living room. They broke in and said the Japanese had bombed Pearl Harbor and destroyed our navy, which had been anchored there in the harbor. I ran to the kitchen, where my mother was, and told her the Japanese sank our navy and we were at war.

I asked her, "Can the Japanese bomb the U.S.?"

She said, "God, I hope not."

Later in the war, my uncle with the 3rd Army sent a V-mail letter home (before the news was made public) and said that the Nazis had torn the skin off the Jewish people and made lamp shades out of the human skin.

The impact the war had on me is that the flag became my "baby blanket."

ROBERT RUNION

I was living in east Tennessee at the ripe old age of eight, so my recollections are from a child's perspective. I do remember when my father came home to announce the bombing of Pearl Harbor. My father, who had recently retired from the U.S. Navy, was pretty upset since he had served in the Pacific Fleet and, of course, was familiar with a lot of the area and ships around Hawaii.

He was recalled to active duty in January 1942, and spent most of that interlude in the South Pacific. I never saw him again until August 1945, just before V-J Day. It was a pretty scary time for me, not knowing just what bombing a ship meant, nor where Hawaii was located—I thought we were being invaded.

I do remember the rationing of just about everything. I remember my mother having to cut corners to keep my sister and me fed, clothed, and housed. She was all by herself and had no job. I recall that we ate a lot of oatmeal and grits during this time.

G. J. FULLER

I remember quite well that day. I was a teenager, and my sister was working for a funeral director about fifteen miles away. His living quarters were over the funeral home, and he had four lovely little boys.

A funeral was scheduled for that day, so I was requested to keep the boys entertained as quietly as possible. We wound up going for a car ride a little later in the day.

When the news came over the radio, everyone seemed to be in a state of shock. I had several close relatives, including three brothers, who would later serve in the military. It certainly was the topic of conversation that day and for weeks to come.

Since then, I've had a husband, son, and several nephews who have served during one war or another.

AVRE PAPST

I was eleven-years-old when Pearl Harbor occurred. I was riding my bike on the "ramp" of a general store/service station in our rural neighborhood. My father was visiting inside the store that Sunday morning, with two or three other neighbors, when the news came over the radio.

The day was clear and bright in Beaver Creek, Oregon. This was exceptional. Usually in December it was rainy.

There was a huge state of uncertainty and fright for the future. Everyone seemed to be asking how this could have happened and saying that the country was in no condition to fight a war because the economy was still in a depression.

My dad went home in his car. He told me to follow him because he wanted me home, not on the road. There was a fear that an assault might occur on the Pacific coast of Oregon. There was an immediate fear of the Japanese who had been our neighbors for years—and they were probably more "Americanized" than I was. They were not to be trusted because of the "sneak attack" on Pearl Harbor. As a child, I immediately began hating the Japanese. Hysteria is the only way I can describe the attitude of the locals when I reflect on the folks there at the store.

My peer group didn't seem to care about the situation. I did care and listened to the adults.

AVIS EMMONS

On December 7, 1941, I was just a teenager living with my parents in Altadena, California, about three miles in the foothills from Pasadena, California. Even though I was young, we were all shocked and angry when we heard the news on the radio. Our neighbors were just as upset.

The Japanese who worked the fruit and vegetable stands at the local market had been acting unfriendly for some time prior to the attack. Another Japanese had a flower shop, and when neighbors went there, the owners would appear from the rear of the shop dusting off their clothes. It was later discovered that the ones doing the dusting had been digging a tunnel for whatever reason. One tried to pass himself off as Chinese.

LOIS KRONEMER

I was just nine-years-old back on that cold Sunday afternoon. We had recently moved to another house and an uncle of mine did paper hanging. This Sunday was the day he was able to come over and do the work with my dad.

While they were working, a neighbor came over and told us to turn on the radio. "There's big news," we were informed. We turned on the radio and heard the news about Pearl Harbor. We really didn't comprehend the meaning of the news, and my father and uncle went back and finished up the job.

My father later went over to my grandparent's house for some reason. He told them of the news. They hadn't heard yet. They weren't sure what it meant either. They didn't know if it meant we were at war or not.

My father's job exempted him from the draft. His company made netting for submarines, and his job was considered essential.

RAYMOND D. PARKINS

I was thirteen-and-a-half-years-old on that fateful Sunday when the Japanese bombed Pearl Harbor. I was at my sister's house in Long Beach, California, having stayed overnight visiting my nephew. He was three years younger than me and more like a younger brother. My father called about noon to ask if we had heard the news of the bombing. We immediately grouped ourselves around a large Silverstone radio to hear scraps of news as it became available.

I remember that my nephew and I soon tired of listening and went into the back yard where my parent's Marmon automobile was parked up on blocks. We immediately made this our plane (a Hellcat) as we pretended to shoot down Jap Zeros. Naturally, as I was the oldest, I was the pilot and my nephew had to be content being the gunner and bringing down several enemy attackers.

I recall on Monday, December 8, my sixth-grade teacher brought in a radio to class so we could hear President Roosevelt's historic "Day of Infamy" speech, as he declared war on the Japanese empire. I remember that it amazed me that one congresswoman (Rankin) voted against the declaration of war.

Our life changed drastically as a result of the war. We had air-raid alerts, a firing of antiaircraft guns along the railroad tracks which ran behind our house, and food and clothing rationing. We had blue stamps for foodstuffs, red for meat, and green for clothing and shoes. Also, gasoline was tightly rationed with most people getting an "A" sticker. This entitled you to three gallons of gas per week.

As it turned out, rationing was the catalyst that launched me on my lifetime occupation. In the summer of 1943, between my graduation from junior high school and entry into high school, I was looking for part-time work and heard that a local supermarket was hiring box boys. I applied and was hired on the spot and put to work immediately. I did not know at the time, but it was the last day of June and ration stamps expired on a six-month basis. For this reason, everyone was bringing in their about-to-expire stamps and the store was packed all day long. The checker to whom I was assigned realized I knew nothing about bagging groceries, so he soon had me tearing ration stamps out of the books for the customers because we could not take any loose stamps. We did not close the store until 9:00 p.m., and I worked about eight-and-a-half hours without a break. I was so tired I didn't think I would be able to ride my bike home. I must have called home when I got the job because I am sure I would have been in big trouble if I hadn't let my folks know where I was and what I was doing. The only reason I could call home was that my sister, who lived with us, worked at Douglas Aircraft and was entitled to a phone.

When that day was over, I expected to be told I was no longer needed. But the manager asked if I could work the next morning. I was told I would make thirty-three-and-a-third cents per hour, and after two weeks I would receive a raise bringing me up to thirty-five cents. Thus started my career in the grocery business, which concluded in 1983, forty years later. I enjoyed every minute.

DON DALE

There are several occurrences in my life that will always stick with me, in that I remember where I was and what I was doing on a certain day, at a certain time.

One was when JFK was assassinated. Another was when FDR died. A big one was when we heard about Pearl Harbor.

I would be nine-years-old in three weeks. We were eating dinner and, as usual, the radio was playing quietly in the background. Suddenly my dad told me to quickly turn the volume up and we heard the news. Food was forgotten, as we listened to every tidbit we could catch.

My older brother was a member of the Louisiana National Guard, and it was announced that all members were to report to their units. He had recently married and this really caused my parents to be very concerned. Even at my age, I sensed that this was different from the movies. This would touch us personally—for real. Christmas 1941 was not the same!

ANNE BELLENGER

I was only thirteen at the time. My parents lived in Miami, Florida. It was Sunday afternoon and we were all sitting on the porch reading the Sunday newspaper. I was reading the comics. The radio was turned on and the announcer interrupted to announce the attack on Pearl Harbor. Being only thirteen, it didn't mean much to me. However, my parents were very upset. I remember my mother saying something about the nephews probably signing up for the armed forces.

In my school (a private school), we sat in the room with the head-mistress while Roosevelt made his famous speech declaring "a state of war." The adults all were so serious. We children really didn't understand.

Later, I learned my cousins signed up for various services. One cousin, Jack Goodwin, who was a lawyer, went into the army and was put into intelligence with Eisenhower's staff. He was a full colonel and was with Ike when they went into Eagle's Nest, Hitler's mountain retreat, at the end of the war. Jack brought home some silver goblets that belonged to Hitler. He gave a set to my parents. Jack did acknowledge Eisenhower's relationship with his female driver.

Two other cousins, Jack and Joseph Farley, joined the navy. Joe was an executive officer, I believe, on the *Saratoga* when it was sunk in the Pacific. He told stories of being in the water for several hours waiting to be picked up.

Another cousin, Joseph Wheeler, was already in the navy, being an Annapolis man. He was a submarine commander during the war. After the war, he went on to be commandant of the sub station at Key West, Florida.

As to our lives during the war, we had rationing, of course. Stamps of all kinds were issued for gas, food, shoes, etc. I still have those stamp books.

When I went off to college my first year (I was sixteen), I had to turn in my ration books to the college. I remember the food we had was mostly substitution for meat—things like macaroni and rice.

Miami was a nice place to live back in the 1940s. We all knew each other and stuck together in our neighborhoods. So many men were away in the service. There was a regular phone network for support amongst our mothers. All the cars had their headlights painted out except for a little strip so that a light could show onto the road. No one drove much anyway because of gas rationing. If one knew the right people, they could buy black market gas coupons. We did. The owner of our gas station sold them, so we bought them.

We also had to use blackout curtains on the windows. There were air-raid wardens who went around acting very self-important with funny helmets, armbands, and flashlights.

I remember the Army Air Force training men on Miami Beach. They gathered on a golf course for a retreat every afternoon. Sometimes we would watch. The movie actor, Clark Gable, trained there as did some others I can't remember.

The army took over many posh hotels on the beach and painted them army khaki inside and out.

Later on in the war, German U-boats were sinking cargo ships on the

East Coast off Miami Beach allowing the flotsam to come ashore. There were all kinds of articles including hatch covers and rotten food. My dog Pep ate too many of the rotten hams that came ashore and it killed her. That was a horrible thing because that dog had been with me such a long time.

Some people collected hatch covers and turned them into tables. They were made out of good mahogany. Sometimes, bodies showed up as well as life rafts with machine gun bullet holes. Sometimes we could see fires from the torpedoed oil tankers. The sky would be so bright. The oil would then come ashore and get all over everything. I had to wash my dog frequently because she went into the water.

In high school we were given the chance to join the Civil Air Patrol as spotters. We took courses in identifying airplanes as silhouettes. We got overseas caps to wear with a CAP patch. We actually did spotting and reporting. Had to take an oath. That's what I was doing when we saw those bodies come ashore on Miami Beach. Can you imagine the effect that had on me as a teenager?

The Coast Guard patrolled the beach at Miami Beach on horses. There was a great fear of spies coming onshore from German submarines.

My mother volunteered with the Red Cross to be a Gray Lady. They worked at the Biltmore Hotel in Coral Gables, Florida, which had been turned into a hospital. They helped the nurses, wrote letters for the men, etc. My mother had been overseas in France with the Red Cross during World War I, so she was a natural for the job.

The main thing I remember now is the total hatred we had for the Japs (as they were called). There were many songs written and records sold about this. One was, "We're Gonna Have to Slap the Dirty Little Jap."

At the end of the war in Europe, I was in Atlanta with my mother buying winter clothes for college. I was sitting at the hotel window looking out when all of a sudden there was this big noise. People went out into the streets and were cheering and jumping around. We went out for a while, but it was so loud and hysterical that we went back into the hotel. What a relief that was. I have never seen so many happy people.

If I had been a little older, I would have joined the navy. I always felt left out because I couldn't do my part for the "war effort."

June Skelton Dickerson

On December 7, 1941, I was ten-and-a-half-years-old and living in Ashland, Wisconsin. My family consisted of my parents and their eight children. On that Sunday I had been ice skating at the outdoor rink. It was just getting dark when I returned home for supper. My mother was in the kitchen. She was crying as she cooked. This frightened me, as I had never seen my mother cry.

I went into the living room where my dad was seated by the radio and listening intently. He finally told me the Japanese had attacked Pearl Harbor and the ship my brother was on, the *West Virginia*, had been bombed and sunk. We had no word about my brother Dean for several weeks. Then we heard he had been injured slightly but was safe. He spent the entire war in the Pacific and came home only after the war was over.

JOANN WINTERS

I was at Washington's headquarters in Valley Forge, Pennsylvania. My mother, father, and myself were talking to the ranger in charge. The radio was on when the announcement came in.

I was almost twelve-years-old and still in school. My father was a mechanical engineer with Westinghouse Electric (Steam Turbine Division). He went out on every victory ship that left the Philadelphia Naval Yard to the breakwater to be sure the engines worked properly. He would also get ship-to-shore messages from ships in distress from as far away as Africa for information on how to fix the engines. They would follow his instructions and be able to get to shore for full repairs.

He was also an air-raid warden and we had blackout practices. I stood in many a line for food stamps and to buy meat.

SHIRLEY COLES

There are those moments in every lifetime that are never and can never be forgotten, even though one's memory can get a bit unreliable as one gets older. Such a moment, for those who lived it, was the day the Japanese bombed Pearl Harbor. Simply telling you where I was, what I heard, and how it impacted my life thereafter will sound like a simple story, but trying to express the visceral effect would take a book of my own.

To make this long story very short, I was thirteen years of age, visiting along with my mother and paternal grandparents, at the apartment of my deceased father's sister. I mentioned that my father was deceased to explain a little bit of the anxiety that befell me. I had no father's lap or arms to comfort and reassure me.

The radio was on, for we had finished having refreshments, and I was listening while the adults continued their conversation at the table. The announcement broke through as though cutting butter with a knife. What we all heard did not fully register for a few moments. If there were comments made, I didn't hear them. My imagination had already gone into high gear and I was trembling at the thought of Japanese planes coming over my country and destroying us with their bombs.

Life was never to be the same after that. I don't know how else it would have been, but the war flavored every aspect of my existence, from seeing family members enlist, to hearing of an uncle who disappeared, presumed killed by the Nazis in Europe, to meeting whom I was to eventually marry, to the music we came to know, the movies, the headlines, the talk of bomb shelters, and keeping the shades drawn in the evening. It was the best of times and the worst of times for a teenaged girl growing up with World War II as a background for her feelings, hopes, and fears.

VESTA LOU HUBBARD

I started a diary when I was quite young and made entries until the early part of 1946. On December 7, 1941, I was fifteen-years-old and living with my parents and an invalid grandmother in a little village in Virginia.

My aunt and uncle had come to visit my grandmother and were sitting in her bedroom with my parents. I was in the kitchen in front of a little mirror putting on a touch of Tangee lipstick while listening to Sammy Kaye on the radio. The program was suddenly interrupted by the announcement that the Japanese had attacked Pearl Harbor.

I went to the bedroom door and asked where Pearl Harbor was.

My aunt spoke first and told me it was in Hawaii. "One of our boys was stationed at Pearl Harbor when he was in the Navy."

When I told them about the attack, they of course went to listen for more news. I asked, "What does it mean?"

My father said only one word, "War."

The rest of the afternoon and evening was a jumble of news, speculation, and attempts to find out more. President Roosevelt met with his cabinet and we were told he would address a joint session of Congress the next day.

A direct quote from my diary went as follows: "A place called Pearl Harbor has been bombed, and my world and my generation can never be the same again."

FLORENCE HOFMANN

My mother, Rena Jensen, and myself were given a ride by Bill Quarter to Fairfield, California, as my brother, David Jensen, was working in Vallejo at the Mare Island Shipyard. That morning was beautiful, clear, and warm. Mother and I visited her friend near the Southern Pacific Depot at Fairfield/Suisun City. The two cities were divided by the railroad.

My mother and I had left her friend and were walking towards the depot, after seeing Bill and David standing near there. Their faces were ashen. They were both of draft age. They told us that the Japanese had bombed Pearl Harbor. Both said that they would not ask for a deferment and would go into the service.

I had a cousin, Alexander Bain, who was stationed on the USS *Medusa* at Pearl Harbor. He survived the war.

Mother and I boarded the train going to Oakland. I remember seeing the bombing and strafing in China by the Japanese on newsreels that were shown at the time—it being before T.V. I also remember looking at *Life* and *Look* magazines of the bombing in China. I was one scared nine-year-old, thinking that the bombing would happen here.

We went by two oil refineries (gas and storage) in West Costa County, which would have been primary targets. I was very happy to get off the train in Oakland, which was about sixty miles away.

The next day, December 8, I went to school in Oakland and all of the children were sent home from school because they didn't have any way to protect the children from an air raid if one occurred.

My eldest brother, David, went to the Pacific and was in the antiaircraft group. He went to Australia, and in May 1942 went to New Guinea and Moritai (a part of the Dutch East Indies group of islands). He arrived home in April 1945.

My younger brother, James Jensen, was a paratrooper, and since he took rapid shorthand, was put in headquarters in London and the Continent. As the war progressed, he ended up in Berlin, where he went into several former concentration camps, getting data from them to forward to Washington, DC. He returned safely in August 1945.

Another cousin, Archie M. Hendricks, was already in the Philippines, as part of the 26th Horse Cavalry. He was killed on or about December 20, 1941. This information I just obtained recently.

A cousin, Ralph Conner, was in the Army Air Corps and was stationed in Nome, Alaska. Our government was sending war materials to the Russian pilots in Alaska. He went to England and bombed German cities.

One other cousin, Gordon Lawler, went to the South Pacific and was in the Seabees, the construction arm of the navy. He returned safely to his home in Lake County, California.

My uncle, Orval Conner, was drafted into the army in 1942 and was going to be a combat engineer. Because he was an older man, he was able to get a discharge. At that time he was stationed at New Orleans, Louisiana. This was the port of embarkation for the troops going to Europe or the Pacific. He had a war essential job and came back to Oakland in the early part of 1943.

I was in Oakland, California, when the war ended and it was a very joyous day.

Nancy Brackmann

It was a cloudy, chilly Sunday afternoon in Kansas City. I was nine-years-old, and we were driving to visit people in another part of the city.

We happened to stop at a Parkview Drug Store at Independence Ave. and Prospect. There was a small wooden radio over the back of the soda fountain. It spoke of Manila being bombed. My only reference to "Manila" was a manila envelope which always seemed to be important—being more than just an ordinary envelope.

People were moving close to the soda fountain to hear better. I knew immediately that this was exceedingly important. "Pearl Harbor" had no meaning for me, but the looks on peoples' faces were enough.

My parents were quiet. Did they know that my two brothers, born in 1922 and 1925, would be called up? They did and they were.

My brother Harold was a tech sergeant, trained in radio, and went to Scotland, England, France, and Germany. My younger brother, Ruell, entered the V-12 navy program and attended Park College in Parkville, Missouri. He served on the cruiser USS *Montpelier* as an ensign.

Both my brothers finished college on the GI Bill at the University of Kansas. One became a journalist, while the other became a lawyer.

Maxine Richards

On December 7, 1941, I was a young teenager living in western Canada (Saskatchewan), and the daughter of a wheat farmer. My parents were Americans living in Canada.

On that infamous Sunday, my sister, some friends, and I had been skating on a neighbor's frozen pond. When we returned home, my parents told us of the bombing of Pearl Harbor and the imminent declaration of war by the United States.

Since Canada had been at war for years (when Poland was invaded in 1939), my friends could not understand my parents' reaction with statements like, "They'll be sorry now," meaning the enemy, "They've got a tiger by the tail," and "Now this war will really get going and won."

World War II really impacted my family. My brother joined the army and was sent to Sicily, Anzio, etc. My sister's husband was sent overseas while she was expecting her first child in February, so I went to Spokane, Washington, to live with her so she wouldn't be alone. I finished my high school education there.

My brother contracted typhoid fever, and for over a month while he was sent to a field hospital in North Africa, we had no news of him. We didn't know if he was dead or alive.

One of my sisters met her future husband in Spokane, waited years for him, got married, and moved to Texas.

My other sister stayed in Canada marrying a Canadian who was 4-F.

I met my husband in Spokane the summer after I graduated high school. We were married in 1947.

World War II really dispersed my family with my brother going to Oregon to live, my sisters in Washington state and Texas, and my other sister remaining in Canada.

RICHARD M. YOUNG

In the 1930s and 1940s, we did a lot of walking. I walked a half a mile down a parish (county) road each morning to catch my school bus which traveled on a state gravel road.

The morning following December 7, 1941, I again was walking my way towards the state road. About half of the way there, my uncle met me walking in the opposite direction as he was heading for my mother and daddy's house. He was a brother to my mother and was a World War I army veteran. He had a newspaper in his hand, *The Times Picayune* out of New Orleans.

He stopped to tell me, "Boy, we are in trouble now."

He showed me the headlines of the paper which nearly filled the entire front page reading: "War Rages in the Pacific as Japan Attacks the U.S."

Well, of course, being only twelve-years-old, I had no idea of what we were to face for the next four, long, war years. I knew it was serious, though, because my uncle had many bad stories about World War I.

My little friends were about as lost as I to what was ahead of us, but we were all a little sad. Many more days like that were ahead of us as we watched brothers and sisters, one by one, leave for the service or war plants.

We spent four years gathering scrap iron, instead of classes many days, and hearing of those we knew killed or wounded.

I finished high school and served in the Korean War, but I never have forgotten those broad headlines on December 7, 1941, nor my uncle's serious concern.

Vera Riley

I was twelve-years-old on December 7, 1941. I was living in Columbia, South Carolina, on the not-to-be-forgotten day, and remember specific details.

As I visualize that occasion, I was at home when I heard the news on the big standing up radio which had large knobs on its front. It was Sunday afternoon and in no time we were dressed and ready to go to church. There, we congregated with our immediate family and our church family. I was petite and wore a skirt and jacket. It was one of my favorite church outfits. It was not cold enough for a heavy, long coat.

The one-building wooden church had a large auditorium with a piano up front. I played for the services at times, and often sang as well, but not that night. There was no sermon, no music, and no formalized meeting at all. Instead, we stood around talking about whether the next target would be the United States.

We talked of those we knew in the service. My uncle was there. He had lived with us for a while and he was important. I didn't know everything that was happening, but I knew I was uneasy about it.

People came in the church for the service who did not know yet. We could hardly wait to tell them the terrible news. They were shocked. They, in turn, would tell others. Our main focus, after all the talking, was that we needed to pray and keep on praying, which we did.

At twelve, I mentally photographed a picture of that scene, which is still vivid in my remembrances. At seventy, I still view that experience with a sense of trepidation and awe.

Imogene Foley

I was fifteen-years-old when Japan bombed Pearl Harbor. It was on Sunday morning, and we heard it on the radio. A lot of neighbors came by. They were all crying because they all had sons in the service.

One neighbor and her two daughters were really crying because her son was on the *Arizona*. Of course, they didn't know that the ship had been turned over. News traveled slowly in those days.

From 1941 to 1944, the war took almost all of the boys out of our class in high school. We graduated with twenty-seven girls and only six boys.

I went to college for one year, then went to Oak Ridge, Tennessee, and got a job making the atomic bomb. My job was to help make the radioactive powder that went into the bomb, which was then shipped out on trains and inserted into the bomb elsewhere.

Pat Vang

I was nine-years-old that awful Sunday of Pearl Harbor. My father's grocery store was quiet that Sunday and just he and I were there with the radio on. Suddenly this bulletin came across saying the Japanese had bombed Pearl Harbor in the Hawaiian Islands. Most Americans didn't even know where Pearl Harbor was or even much about Hawaii back then. People were asking where it was, and the ESSO (now EXXON) Oil Company began to publish huge war maps of all the different theaters of war, and were hung all over everywhere, as Americans learned geography fast.

My dad knew what the Japanese bombing meant, and he had tears in his eyes. I was scared, as I never saw dad cry before.

I asked him what it meant and he said, "War, little girl, war with the Japanese."

I was nine and it was a much more innocent world than we have today. I had never known war so I asked, "Is it real bad, Daddy?"

He looked so sad, this old veteran of World War I, and he said, "Yes baby, very, very bad. A lot of good men will die. That is what war is."

Soon my uncle came rushing in and some of the men that lived near the store did as well, I think, to discuss this terrible event. My young uncle said, "I have to go enlist," to my dad and told him he'd have to take care of my grandmother and the farm. Dad just shook his head "yes" as he and his younger brother hugged with tears.

I just sat there, stunned, and listened to all the men talk, not understanding it all. Not all those men seemed to understand either. No one could believe a tiny country like Japan would take on the USA and bomb our largest naval base in the Pacific. And to think no one had seen it coming. All of the men kept saying, "How did this happen," over and over as if in shock.

I think it was the next day when President Roosevelt came on the radio to tell the people that we had officially declared war with the empire of Japan and made his famous "a date which will live in infamy" speech about the awful bombing on Pearl Harbor.

In the next few weeks, America came close to losing the war on the many Pacific islands, as we were not ready for war. But, our people made us ready fast. Our country had never seen such a burst of togetherness and industry as the American people displayed during the years from December 1941 until 1945. Those were our finest hours. Our men and boys proved their devotion to their country and cause and our people stood behind them 100 percent.

Everything changed almost over night all over the country as every industry, every home, every city and town geared up for war. Women who never worked outside the home now had to, as the men that were not too old or sick virtually disappeared into the military right away. Women's lives in America changed forever with that act.

Women began to run the country, as well as their homes. Our traveling, eating, and living habits also changed virtually overnight with the rationing of almost everything. We also had blackout curtains and air-raid wardens in even the smallest towns.

There was suddenly a new middle class with the high wages paid in the defense plants. Soldiers and people who never dreamed of owning things like refrigerators, TVs, new cars, and new homes suddenly had money in those later war years. However, that first year was touch and go. We learned from posters on walls and on the radio to not talk about the war for fear the enemy might be listening. We learned to sing lots of war songs like "You're a Sap, Mr. Jap," "Uncle Sam Is Gonna Spankee" along with songs about war heroes like Colin Kelly and "Praise the Lord and Pass the Ammunition." Hollywood also cranked out dozens of war movies almost at once.

It was a sad and scary time too, as every month someone you knew seemed to get killed or wounded in the war. In the towns across America, boards, with the names of our dead and wounded veterans, sprung up in the towns' parks. It was a time of enormous patriotism and faith in God and in America.

Few people had TVs back then, but everybody had a radio. At 6 p.m. every night, the news commentator came on and all American families pulled up to the radio and listened as he said in his very stentorian tone, "There is good news tonight," or "There is bad news tonight."

We went to the movies to see Movietone News pictures of the war. In school, all of the children paid a dime a week for bond stamps. When you got a full book, you received a savings bond that helped the boys in the war, so even the kids were involved. They also gathered milkweed pods to make parachute silk and we filled hundreds of burlap bags to supply the military.

Suddenly, America was no longer just a lot of little rural towns and big cities, but overnight we pulled together to become one big city. It was wonderful. We had so much pride in our country, its flag, and its servicemen and women.

I am grateful I grew up then because it gave me a very solid foundation to grow from and things to believe in for the rest of my life. Mine may be the last generation that was sure of who they were in America. Today, my life is still based on the things I learned to believe in during those years of war. Nothing since those years has seemed quite as good, or the same. I liked it better when we were all proud to be Americans, not just one or two days a year but right up front, every day, and not ashamed to say it. That's when God, honor, duty, flag, and country really meant something that counted.

Pearl Harbor changed our country forever. It was a day that will live in infamy, but it was also the day America took off her rose-colored glasses and grew up. We didn't know it then, but our world and life had changed forever on that fate-filled day of December 7, 1941. We lost a lot more than planes, ships, and men. We would never be a young, innocent, naive country again.

ANNA FRIEANDT

I was attending the annual Methodist Church Conference of Kansas, which was being held in the "Old Forum" in Wichita, Kansas. While the bishop of the Kansas Methodist Church was preaching, a little boy came up to him with a note. From this message he announced that Pearl Harbor had been bombed by the Japanese.

The adults started to cry. I remember, I was fifteen-years-old and did not know what Pearl Harbor was. My brother was fourteen and did not know either.

My future husband (1947), Warren Frieandt, was walking to a drugstore to buy a Sunday paper when he heard the news on the street from people walking by. The next day he enlisted in the navy. He had just turned eighteen-years-old. He was discharged in 1946.

LYNN POND

I had turned twelve years of age in March 1941. While I was in Canada, at a fishing camp in July of that year, my mother gave birth to her fourth child. A week later, my father, a forty-year-old reserve officer in the (then) Army Air Corps, was called into active service as a "shavetail" (second lieutenant). He reported to Wright-Patterson Field in Dayton, Ohio. It would be a year before Dad was able to save enough money to move us to Springfield to join him.

On the morning of December 7, 1941, my mother's brother drove to the flat in River Forest (Illinois) in which we six—mother, dad's father, and we four children—were quartered to take us to his home in Oak Park to spend the day with his family. My aunt had fixed a large dinner geared towards pleasing us children—fried chicken with all the trimmings. Prior to sitting down to eat, my uncle turned on his large console radio to a music station to, "aid the digestive juices," as he phrased it. Shortly after we began to enjoy my aunt's cooking, the music was interrupted with the first announcement of the attack on Pearl Harbor. The adults deserted the dining table to cluster around the radio. I was shocked to see my mother begin to cry. The adults never did finish their dinners.

We three children were alarmed to see our mother cry. Her explanation that our country would now be at war and that Dad might be in danger held little meaning for us at the time. Actually I probably remember the following day and FDR's "Day of Infamy" speech better than I remember Pearl Harbor day itself. It was that speech which made me more clearly realize that we were at war, and gave me some vague inkling that life was not going to go on as it had. I still remember the timbre and clarity with which FDR intoned "day of infamy."

Throughout my school years, from that point on, I would be the only student whose father, instead of a brother, was a member of the armed forces. It did bring me a few school privileges such as being able to leave at 2:00 instead of 3:30 each day to help Mother with my baby sister. A number of my fellow students lost brothers, and were more objects of morbid curiosity by their peers than of finer feelings. At that age, the youngsters didn't fathom even the thought of death.

Dad came through the war unscathed, although at one point he was missing for two months in the Aleutians, of all places. By the end of the war, he had attained the silver oak leaves of a Lieutenant colonel, and was offered a permanent commission to stay in active service, which Mother forced him to refuse.

Since Mother was ill much of the time from worrying about Dad, I sort of became a surrogate mother to my baby sister, the family shopper, sometime cook, laundress, and maker of the butter. To this day, just a whiff of sour cream (with which I made the butter) makes me nauseous.

I really don't think that the attack on Pearl Harbor meant as much to citizens under eighteen. Young people are very self-centered, and war is not really something they can fathom, especially when it does not affect them directly. Sure, we were frightened by the thought of possibly being bombed, but blackouts were more an inconvenience than a necessity to our way of thinking. Learning about battles that we lost was worrisome, and parents tried to reassure us that the United States and her allies would prevail—and maybe did too good of a job trying to keep us carefree.

DIXIE CLARK

When I tell friends that I remember Pearl Harbor, I am usually told that I couldn't possibly. I was nineteen-months-and-one-day-old, having been born May 6, 1940.

I do not remember all of the details. What I do remember is burned into my soul. My mother was ironing. I do not remember who else was at home with us, but there were other adults there. I was the only child.

My mother always ironed in a small room where she kept a radio. When she ironed, I could not go in there. She used a flat iron that had to have a heat source. We did not get an electric iron until after the war, around 1945.

Our house was at Ross Gravel Company located back in the woods from Cravens, Louisiana, near the still-active army installation called Fort Polk.

My mother came running out of the ironing room squealing, "The Japs have bombed Pearl Harbor! The Japs have bombed Pearl Harbor!" While I did not know what her words meant at that moment, I sensed deep fear. Babble broke out amongst the adults who felt sure Jap planes would fly over Camp Polk, wiping it out—and us.

My family usually went to town about once a month to buy groceries (whatever we didn't raise or grow) and to see a movie. I remember those black-and-white newsreels that told me, and everyone in our world, just what the bombing of Pearl Harbor really meant.

ERNESTINE PINA McGOLDRICK

It was a sunny morning that December 7, 1941, a happy and carefree time for this sixteen-year-old. My girlfriend was over for a Sunday dinner that was being prepared by my mother. The radio was playing loudly—it was Benny Goodman, our favorite. Then came the interruption. The excited announcer said, "Pearl Harbor has been bombed." The question everyone asked was, "Where is Pearl Harbor?" We were unsophisticated teenagers—if they didn't teach it at school, we sure didn't learn geography at home. The Hawaiian Islands were a territory of ours, we knew that. It was not a time of air transportation. To get there, you had to take a ship. Only the rich could afford that. It didn't sink in. We laughed and joked, then had our usual Sunday dinner.

We went downtown to the movies, and then it hit us. This was not something we had ever experienced. While we were sitting in the theater, there were announcements for sailors, soldiers, and marines to report to their ships or units immediately. Seeing the houselights go on and all of these young men hurriedly leaving the theater, and the hush that fell, you could hear just the footsteps. No one spoke. No one could say anything. It was so confusing, so scary.

We figured it was best to go home. The warmth and reassurance of our parents telling us that everything would be O.K. was needed.

When we left the theater, out in the street, we saw more soldiers, sailors, and marines running back to their bases in an excited fashion. Little did they know that it was going to be a long, cruel war for them. Just the street lights were on. The city had gone dark. Gone were the marquee lights, the store lights, and the blinking neon signs.

The next day was even worse. Back at school the girls were crying because their brothers and sweethearts were in the service—some in Hawaii. Boys were boasting that they were joining up to go fight the Japs.

An assembly was called, and we all gathered in the auditorium. There was a small radio on the stage. Remember, this was an unsophisticated time in the life of this teenager. There was no sound system, just a small radio in the middle of the stage. Two thousand students, staff, and teachers, and not a sound could be heard. All our straining ears were listening to President Roosevelt declare war on Japan.

Life was not the same anymore. It was no longer carefree. It was a time for good-byes, a time for saving tin cans and foil from the cigarette packages, a time of rationing and saving that shoe stamp for your first pair of high heels to wear to graduation.

Do I remember that day! It changed many lives, it changed our city. It robbed me of part of my youth. How could you remain irresponsible when they were drafting your friends right out of high school? One day you'd say good-bye, the next you'd go to church and see your friend's name with a gold star next to it.

The war was long, hard, and a dark shadow over all of us until the day the boys came home. In the meantime, longshoremen became rich, landlords were kings, employers begged you to work for them, and the movie theaters went on for twenty-four hours showing terrible English movies.

My younger brother joined the navy and saw action in the Pacific. Letters to friends were returned blackened out, meaning that they were lost in action.

Yes, I remember Pearl Harbor and when it was bombed on that Sunday a long, long time ago.

3

HOLDING DOWN THE HOMEFRONT

In the early 1940s, with military operations in full swing, the United States faced a labor shortage. The greatest majority of men, ages eighteen to thirty-five, were occupied with military service. The need was never greater for a strong, well-stocked workforce. Aside from the everyday factory responsibilities, the war effort required aircraft, munitions, raw materials, foodstuffs, and so forth, and the demand wasn't being met. That incredible need gave birth to the concept, then reality, of Rosie the Riveter—the new look in America's workforce.

Norman Rockwell captured this likeness in his *Saturday Evening Post* cover art. The War Production Board as well as the U.S. Crop Corps, a subdivision of the Emergency Farm Labor Service, produced similar posters displaying the able-bodied woman aiding the war effort.

The exceptional sacrifices of American women at that time have yet to be equaled. This truly was American women's finest hour.

By 1944, nearly 3 million women, mothers to 4 million American children, were now workforce employees.[1] One in three women in defense-related jobs had previously been full-time housewives and mothers.[2] Still, maintaining a household and holding down a job simultaneously became a new and exhausting experience.

Women who were not able, or had the luxury of remaining stay-at-home mothers, found other outlets to aid in the U.S. war effort. Many volunteered at the Red Cross, canned garden produce, sold war bonds, or donated their time to women's auxiliaries.

Women found that during the war their time and skills were valuable in the formerly male-dominated labor force. The women in America, and their family lives, would never be the same.

ERMA HARRIS

On December 7, 1941, I was sixteen-years-old. I was at work at the Dairy Lane Soda Fountain on Main Street in Porterville, California. My bosses, Lottie and Louise, had the radio on in the kitchen. It blared with the news of Pearl Harbor. It scared me to death. I was crying as Louise, a woman in her late fifties, hugged me.

A family friend, the same age as me, Bill Delco of Coalinga, California, said, "I'm joining the Marines." He did. He was shot at in the Philippines and lived. A battlefield commission made him a major. He walked the sands of Iwo Jima and lived. He retired a Lieutenant colonel in 1980. We have been friends for over fifty-seven years.

I also survived the war. My sharecropper father became an invalid in 1940. I was married in 1944 to a man in the Army Air Corps. I knew him eleven months when he shipped out on December 15, 1944. I was pregnant. My forty-four-year-old mother passed away on March 1, 1945, leaving me four months pregnant and with four little brothers. So, at the age of twenty-years-old, I was responsible for the care of five children and a bedridden father. I went back to work when my baby was ten-days-old. I had to have money to buy food.

My remembrance of Pearl Harbor is as clear today as it was on December 7, 1941. I lived through World War II. Thank God it was over in 1945.

MARTHA KUNKEL

On December 7, 1941, I was at home in Muncy, Pennsylvania. My fiancé and I were going to have a small party to announce our engagement. We were actually going to get engaged on Christmas Day, but chose December 7 to announce it. Before we had the chance to declare our good news, the report broke on the radio. People didn't want to leave the radio and its news, so we postponed our announcement.

My fiancé was going to be drafted, so he joined instead so he could go into the Air Corps, which is what he wanted. He ended up having to go in on January 1st. The night before, New Year's Eve, we went to a fancy hotel and danced the night away. We loved to dance. The next day his parents were going to take him out to Illinois to join the Air Corps.

Two years later, on the spur of the moment when he got a leave, he said he was coming home and we needed to be married within two weeks. That's all of the time he had off. My mother went to the cupboard and dumped out a big red jar of dimes she had been saving forever. She had

$50 in there which was enough to buy a wedding gown. We got married in a church with all the satin.

Several years later, I came across the bill for our wedding night stay at a fancy hotel in Williamsport. In 1943, the cost for our overnight stay came to something like $11. Our meal for that evening was $2.65—for the both of us! And this was gourmet.

During the war years, my last name was Von Neida. That was not a good name to have in those days. Hearing that name raised a few eyebrows. People would hear "Von" and would ask if I was German. I worried that I might be excluded from some social functions because of that. Through a little research I found out that my name was French not German. The name was spelled with a capital "V" and not a lower case "v" as it would be if it was of German derivation.

VERA V. HARVEY

I was born in Twin Falls, Idaho, in 1910, and moved to Buhl, Idaho, in 1914. On December 7, 1941, we were on the patio of the home of Angelo and Palma Bullara. My son, Craig, was six-months-old. We were listening to the radio when it was announced that Pearl Harbor had been bombed by the Japanese. We thought it was a hoax.

When I returned to work, blackout shades had been installed on all of the hospital's windows. If the siren blew, we worked by flashlights.

We had a Japanese American doctor and R.N. on staff. The authorities picked them up at work. They had the choice of going into the service or to the concentration camp at Hunt, Idaho. They went into the service. Some of the Hunt buildings still exist and are used as storage or for cattle.

The men who were at home organized neighborhood watches looking for uncovered windows and searched the sky for planes outlined by the searchlights. When the plane had been identified, the siren became still.

In our Montebello home we installed blackout curtains. We had an inside hall stocked with food, water, medicine, blankets, and chairs. We went there when the sirens blew. In our backyard we had a victory garden and raised chickens.

ANNETTE LEVEILLEE

This is the true story of Staff Sergeant Alcide Leveillee who signed up at the age of seventeen. He had to have his father sign the papers to enlist in the U.S. Army. When the news came that Pearl Harbor was bombed by the Japanese on December 7, 1941, my fiancé and I were sitting in his automobile listening to the radio at 10:20 p.m. We had just left the Hills-grove Skating Rink and were sitting in the car while drinking a chocolate milk shake and eating fries outside the snack bar.

My husband to be had just graduated from Country High School in Rhode Island when we heard of the attack on Pearl Harbor. Some of our school friends were killed there. It was a sad year for us. I was unable to finish the twelfth grade because my father was working on a roof when the gutter gave way, breaking both of his feet.

I was hired to go work at a Speidel Jewelry firm and was promoted to supervisor in three months' time. My weekly pay helped out financially at home.

The day after the news, my future husband left his job at Brown and Sharp Tool Factory. He visited me and told me that he'd be leaving to go enlist at Fort Benning, Georgia, to fight for our country. He said he'd be under the command of General Patton.

At Fort Benning, he got all of his clothing issued to him including his helmet. Under it, he carried my picture from our engagement.

The day before D-Day, he was shot and injured while in the air after he jumped out of his plane. Then he was taken prisoner by the Germans. Losing thirty-five pounds in three months, all he was fed daily was one slice of bread, made with flour mixed with sawdust, and one cup of chicken broth. The German people didn't have enough food to feed our soldiers, so they would shoot seven men a week because of the food short-age.

My husband was to be the next one to die the following week, and he prayed constantly to the Lord to spare his life. A miracle happened! A French underground man appeared at the prison fence and asked my husband if he could speak French. He answered in the affirmative. This underground man brought him a change of clothes and helped him es-cape the prison camp. He was brought to a Red Cross shelter to get med-ical help.

When he was able to fight again, he caught up with his 101st Airborne Infantry Division where he fought in Normandy. There, he was wounded by a hand grenade thrown at him. It removed the flesh near his heart. Again he returned to the hospital for more treatment. When he healed, he again looked for his company and fought in Bastogne out of a fox-hole.

At that time, I was living with my parents, which was a blessing, be-cause I had someone to come home to. One day my mom's phone rang. She answered it and let out a yell. She couldn't believe it was my hus-band's voice. He asked where I was and she told him I was at work. He had her promise not to tell me that he would phone at 4:00 p.m.

As usual, I came home tired and sat down to have a cup of coffee. The phone rang and my mom told me to answer it, but I told her to take a message. She said, "I think you should answer it." So, out of respect to my mom, I answered it and it was my husband.

He said so cheerfully, "Hi honey! Pack your bags as I'll be home soon and we are going to be sent by the government to Martha's Vineyard for two months. I'm being sent there to recuperate from the wounds I've received." I thought I'd pass out from shock after getting through the mistaken telegrams of him being dead.

I'm not a nurse, but I spent twenty years caring for his wounds. God was good and spared his life until he was fifty-four years old. He died in 1979. We would be celebrating over sixty years of married life if he had survived.

I feel so bad about our young servicemen going to war. No one knows what that's like but a mom who has babies, and along comes another war—so unnecessary.

Naomi Broyles

On December 7, 1941, it was a quiet Sunday afternoon for me in Dallas, Texas. The news came over the radio and I was in shock! I could not believe it at first and kept listening to the radio reports until I finally accepted that this was true.

I called my mother to ask if she had heard about this. We were both in disbelief and were wondering what would happen next.

I was nineteen-years-old and working on my first job as a clerk at an office at the Cotton Exchange Building in Dallas. Monday, December 8, I was shocked again when I saw FBI agents taking the Japanese traders out of the building. There were a large number of Japanese on the trading floor. This took place shortly after the start of business in the exchange.

My life was drastically changed afterwards. My husband was in the air force in central Texas at the time and was shipped to Europe with the 8th AF in late 1943. I joined the Women's Army Corps (WAC) and was stationed at Hq. 3rd AFB in Tampa, Florida. He was furious for my enlisting and we almost broke up over it. He came back in 1945 and we did get back together. He has been out of my life now for some time, but I'll never forget those years.

Iris Bancroft

In 1941, I was nineteen years of age and a soprano in three choirs at Fourth Presbyterian Church in Chicago, Illinois. On that fateful day, I had gone to Wimpy's for a hamburger during the break between the morning service and the vespers' recital. On my way back down Michigan

Boulevard, south from Chicago Avenue, I heard the news as a newsboy began to hawk his papers.

I remember a feeling of excitement accompanied by an unexplainable feeling of guilt. Yet, I was still a bit breathless when I reached the church and hurried up to the choir rehearsal room. Still responding to my initial excitement, I blurted out my news and paused, waiting for the choir director's response.

He was silent for a moment. "There's nothing about war to celebrate, Iris." His voice was solemn and I knew he was right. But I could not quite suppress my exhilaration. My life to date had been relatively uneventful. So had my future. Now, suddenly, I knew anything could happen. The new possibilities ahead were impossible to ignore. Through the rest of the day, I allowed the excitement to bubble.

To a small degree, that feeling of newness persisted throughout the years of the war. I married my boyfriend and, in time, went with him to the train station when he left to join the navy. And through it all, I felt as if I were the heroine in a romantic movie. My life seemed more meaningful, my actions more important. The background of the war—which never hurt me as it did many others—imparted a specialness to life.

I suppose it still does that service for the young, even today, when war is even more destructive than it was in the 1940s. I wonder if we can ever change that. I hope we can. When I look back at all the lives that were harmed by wars since 1941, I realize that until we can strip war of its glamour, we will continue to have young people willing to surrender themselves to its lure of "specialness and unexplored possibilities."

EVELYN MILLER ANDERSON

When I heard the news that the Japanese attacked Pearl Harbor, I was performing with my sisters at a benefit show and dance. We were the Six Miller Sisters from Lansdowne, Maryland. We performed at USOs, army bases, Merchant Marine rest homes, etc. We were four teenagers and two younger sisters.

Our mother made our costumes and our father drove our station wagon with all of our instruments, costumes, our brother, parents, and the six of us Miller sisters. We played music, sang, and tap danced all through the war years. When the war was over, we disbanded and several of us married.

SYLVIA SUMMERS

I was a senior at Palo Verde High School in Blythe, California. I lived with my parents on a small farm on North Arrowhead Boulevard. I worked after school and on Saturdays at the local Sprouse Reitz store. The day was clear and sunny, and the temperature was cool, but not cold for December. That morning we turned on the radio and caught the early news. The Japanese had attacked Pearl Harbor. One of my classmates, Louis Stockton, had gone down on the USS *Arizona*. Louis had enough credits to graduate and left school early to join the navy. Immediately after boot camp, he had shipped out on the *Arizona*.

Our farm was far enough from town that we could not hear the sirens when they sounded. Around 10 a.m. on that morning, a girl I worked with at the store, who lived in town, came out to tell me that our store burned during the night. We had been getting in merchandise for the Christmas holiday sales, and just the day before had unpacked crates of chinaware. The store was completely gutted and the new chinaware was one large lump of glass where the storeroom had been.

The war made big changes in all our lives. My dad, being a farmer, got a few more ration stamps for gasoline than some people did, but we all were very careful about driving and used what we had very sparingly. My older sister, who was living at home, and three of her girlfriends signed up to go to Fort Ord in Monterey to work at the PX. I still had a half year of school to finish so I stayed home and continued to work at the store after it was redone. Within two months we were restocking and getting ready to reopen.

Later, I went to work at a local beauty shop, where I spent two years as a junior operator, before going out to Los Angeles to take the test for my operator's license. I worked at the same beauty shop all during the war. I saw the troops come and go on their desert training around Blythe. I watched the bombers do their training from the Air Force base on the West Mesa. I saw the fighter pilots training on the North Mesa from Morton Air Academy.

The woman I worked for at the shop was not much older than I was, even though she had been married and had two small boys. We often worked late, sometimes far into the night. One weekend, over 3,000 men were released for a weekend pass. These boys had been training out in the desert around Blythe and were starved for baths, milk, fresh fruit, haircuts, and shaves. My boss and I stayed at the shop until 3 a.m. giving haircuts and shampoos, as did every other barbershop in town. Only those who had closed up and gone home at the usual hour were not to have this heartwarming experience. They were so hungry for someone to talk to, someone to just listen. On Monday morning, the stores were almost bare of anything edible—no soda pop, no beer, no fresh fruit, or vegetables. The sidewalk trash cans were overflowing and the walks were stacked with empty containers, but no one cared. We just cleaned up the mess and went about our daily chores.

Our lives were far from what you'd call normal, but all in all, we suffered very little compared to our servicemen. My boss and I happened to be in Los Angeles on a buying trip when the war was declared over. The celebrating was unbelievable. The people were dancing in the streets, all of the stores were closed, and everybody joined in the celebration. Some streets were blocked off completely. You could only drive at a snail's pace, if at all. I think that was one of the happiest days of my life.

I did a lot of growing up in those war years. I think most of us did. We never believed that something of that proportion could hit so close to home. The city of Blythe had very few young men left. At one time, people were asked to bring in pictures of their servicemen and all were placed in a local store window. A local photographer took pictures of the window and I still have those pictures. I plan to try to identify all the photos and have them mounted and framed for use in our local museum, along with a list of local boys who were in the service. That was a time I don't think any of us should forget.

Dorothy Pollard Samson

I had gone home to Marshall, Missouri, for the weekend, and my fiancé, Walter Pollard, and I announced our engagement at noon on December 7, 1941. During our jubilation, someone turned on the radio and we heard the news that Pearl Harbor had been bombed.

We went back to Kansas City. I was in X-ray training at St. Luke's Hospital and Walt worked at Remington Arms. He was drafted and left February 22 for Jefferson Barracks in St. Louis, where he received his basic training. Then he was sent to Kansas City for radio school because he was in the Air Force. He was sent to several other places, then back to St. Joseph, Missouri, to teach.

We were married, then he was sent overseas. We have a son and a granddaughter. Walt died one week short of our fiftieth wedding anniversary.

Lila Taylor

I vividly remember the attack on Pearl Harbor, Sunday, December 7, 1941. I was twenty-four-years-old. We had been having a birthday dinner for my oldest brother, Robert L. Taylor, who turned twenty-two that day. We were all sitting around the table when the unbelievable news came on the radio. We were stunned.

All through my schooling, I had been taught that there would be no more wars after World War I. We all knew how horrible war was—unthinkable.

We were a large family—five boys and three girls. My four older brothers enlisted in the navy and they all came back.

LOLA FINLEY

On Sunday morning, December 7, 1941, the news came blaring over the radio: "Japanese attack Pearl Harbor!" We heard it early, before breakfast, in the small town of Coquille, Oregon.

We were eighteen miles from the Pacific coast, seventeen from the port of Coos Bay, and we immediately plunged into frantic activity. In our "touched off" imagination, some reported hearing guns, pictured troop ships docking at Coos Bay, and wondered if we'd be captured in a few hours.

We scrambled to hang blankets over our windows at night, the night shift at the local plywood plant shut down, and we stayed close to home by the radio.

My generation of young adults hadn't experienced war before. We had heard about "the war to end all wars," World War I, and Kaiser Bill, but I must admit none of it seemed very real or close.

On that memorable day, December 7, 1941, we were plunged into the reality of war whether we were ready or not. The war that started with the Japanese bombing of Pearl Harbor was close, too close. Not knowing what to expect day by day, we constantly had new experiences. We became acquainted with blackout curtains, security checks, and rearranged work schedules.

It was both tragic and exciting, scary and exhilarating. It was serious, but there were moments when it had its lighter sides. Many times we laughed when we felt like crying. We lived through heartbreaking good-byes and wonderful reunions. Days of anxious wondering why the letters didn't come were punctuated by times when sweet letters of promise arrived almost daily.

We learned new meanings to the words cooperation, sacrifice, "the war effort," and rationing. Our shoes were made of paper, and silk stockings were replaced by rayon. Wooden toys were a poor substitute for metal. We saved our toothpaste tubes to trade in for new filled ones.

Auto factories converted to building wartime Jeeps. New cars were almost nonexistent. We bought a deluxe, 1932 Packard for $75.00. It was so big we almost needed a phone to contact backseat passengers. As gasoline rationing came on, we couldn't keep it filled at the rate of eight miles to the gallon. Or was it eight gallons to the mile? So we traded it in on a 1934 Chevy.

Tires, sugar, shoes, as well as canned foods were rationed. When our son came along, it took most of our canned food stamps to get Gerber's baby food for him.

My husband's cousin owned a grocery store nearby and he sometimes alerted us to nonrationed foods. He was a shrewd businessman. I remember the time he took a case of sauerkraut juice from the storeroom, where he stored it, because it was a poorly selling item. He stacked the cans up, pyramid style, in the middle of the store and put a sign on the stack saying "Ration-Free Limit. Two Cans Per Customer." People began to carry out as many cans as they could wheedle out of him. He laughed with my husband about it. That night my husband brought home four cans of sauerkraut juice. He explained it this way, "It was a bargain and Jack let me have four cans."

My husband was a young pastor. Every day we were faced with different and challenging problems from brokenhearted mothers and fathers, wives and sweethearts. Tragedy affected nearly every family in some way. Our own family was notified of the serious wounding of my brother in Germany three weeks after it happened. The longest week I can remember was between that telegram and the sound of my brother's voice on the telephone. He was in an army hospital in Auburn, California. He said that although his legs were paralyzed, he was O.K. and getting treatment. He never regained the use of his legs.

A problem, however, that we found no solution for, has given us many laughs through the years. We did realize how serious it was to the person at the time, though. It was near midnight when the telephone rang. Amid her sobs, the woman said, "Pastor, something terrible has happened. Can you come?" She was a member of our church, a dear lady, a little past middle age. We couldn't imagine what happened, and she was so beside herself she couldn't tell us.

When my husband got to her house, she finally managed to tell him someone had stolen her sugar rationing book with all her sugar coupons.

"Lady," my husband told her, "You don't need me, you need a policeman. I'm sorry, I can't help you with this problem."

I don't remember what happened. I think she found it where she'd hidden it. Now, whenever one of us starts to make a giant-sized hill from a tiny mound, the other will say, "What's the matter, did you lose your sugar book?"

MARIE FAGAN

Around the time of December 7, 1941, I was living in Philadelphia. I had been married for three years, and my husband was employed at the Philadelphia Navy Shipyard. I was in the house when I heard what I thought to be a bit of a commotion outside. When I looked out the window, there was a young boy hawking newspapers. When I went out and looked, the paper read, "War Declared!" I don't really remember what kind of day it was, but I'm sure it was a typical winter's day. I don't re-member it raining when we went out to get the paper, though. I do re-member all of the neighbors coming out to buy a copy, and we all started talking about it.

I was truly worried about my husband because he worked at the ship-yard. As it turned out, he was exempt from the draft because his job was classified as strategic to the war effort. I told my husband when he came home from work, but he had already heard the news. I was also worried because I just had our first baby in September. At that point I wasn't sure if the world would end tomorrow after hearing that news or not.

Afterwards, I do remember all of the ration books. It didn't matter how much money you had. If you didn't have your coupon book, you couldn't buy meat.

ANNE ZINDA

On December 7, 1941, I was in my kitchen baking cookies for my nephews who were in the service. It was a dreary day, especially after hearing the horrifying news. My husband was taking a nap. When I told him the news, he was shocked. He was at an age that he could be drafted, and we had three young children. He had a brother killed in World War I.

We had six nephews in the service. One was killed in Europe and one died in a prisoner of war camp.

ARLENE SCHWARTZ

I lived in Philadelphia on 54th St. at the time. I had a husband and a son who was one-and-a-half-years-old at the time. I was in the living room and had the radio on. I was pregnant at the time with my second child. I was thinking of my husband and knew that we were going to get into the war.

My husband went in the service in 1942. His mom and dad were liv-ing with us at the time and they heard the news. They had four sons and two of them went in. Frank went in the air force and my husband was in the infantry in Europe. Frank did fifty bombing missions over occupied Europe and came home in 1944. My husband was wounded in the Battle of the Bulge in December 1944. He was hospitalized in England and came home in 1946.

4

IN THE LOWER 48

In 1941, the United States was still in the throes of the Great Depression. The country's population had risen to slightly more than 132 million.[1] The birth rate, however, was still considered in the lower range when compared to the decade before the Depression began. The median age for the average American was twenty-nine years of age compared with thirty-five around the millennium.[2] A person's average life expectancy in the early 1940s was just sixty-four years.[3]

Jobs were still at a premium, yielding an average annual income of nearly $1,450.00.[4] That figure was only slightly higher than the pre-Depression average yearly income of $1,400.00.[5]

The country's Gross National Product (GNP) was fifty times smaller that its modern-day counterpart.[6] Only 8 percent of the GNP was used for welfare programs compared with roughly 18 percent today.[7] That figure is surprising, considering that the economic adversity of today pales in comparison to that during the Depression.

Style of living, even in those times of misfortune, was in a state of revolution. The number of farms was in decline from its peak of a half-decade earlier. With the modernization of America's roads through government projects such as the WPA, rail traffic was on the downturn from its mid-1920s–30s peak.[8]

In the 1940s, the modernization of modes of communication as just beginning to make the world a smaller place. Actually, there were more post offices in the United States at that time than there are today. They annually ferried twenty-nine billion pieces of mail at three cents per standard letter.[9]

Twenty-three million telephones were in operation (households and businesses), confirming that a fair amount of the thirty-six million U.S. homes still did without them.[10] Finally, radio stations dotted the landscape at slightly less than 1 thousand in number across the United States.[11]

As a result of this modernization, in 1941, few U.S. homes were totally sheltered from the outside world. All of these conveniences led to a fairly rapid dissemination of the news that America was now at war.

KATHLEEN LOVETT

I was out on the farm in northeast Ohio with my family. I don't recall if it was from the radio or the newspaper that I heard about Pearl Harbor being bombed with many of our ships and boys there. The death toll was very high, and ships were destroyed or sunk. Japan was the one to give us the excuse that was needed to turn our "stay out of it" attitude around. The First World War was still too fresh in our minds and the losses still weighed heavily on our hearts.

I walked around in a daze or trance. I couldn't get over the shock of it all. I kept saying, "Japan. Japan did it to us." Somehow we hadn't given Japan much thought. We watched every move Hitler and Mussolini were making in Europe.

That seemed far removed from us. My dad, who was a veteran from World War I, just fell apart as he knew how terrible it could be. He was scared because he had sons of draft age. The older folks looked at all the horrible things that could happen, telling themselves, "We are not ready to go fight a big war. We need ships, planes, bombs. They bombed all of our ships. We are not prepared." Everyone was in an emotional state. We tried to handle our grief and fear in our own way.

Most of the people we knew were immigrants like ourselves with their American-born families. We still had ties and family in the countries Hitler was taking over. Our hearts were heavy with worry for those left behind. We surely didn't want to send our children into war, maybe fight our own people, and possibly lose them too.

Most people in our area listened to President Roosevelt's fireside chats and knew we had to help England, but he would not declare war unless the people were behind him. We younger folks felt we would have to help England, she couldn't hold out for much longer. We knew that if Hitler and Mussolini kept taking one country after another and England fell, they would surely turn their sights on us.

With the Pearl Harbor bombing, President Roosevelt, at last, had his good reason to declare war, which he did. In no time at all the people rallied behind him. We felt he would get us through it and we had faith we could do it, and do it we did.

However, the cost was very high in lives lost. The gold stars indicating that a loved one had fallen fighting for his or her country's freedom started appearing in the windows of our homes all over the country. As I passed, I would bow my head in sympathy. It was a sad time.

JEREMIAH CAMERON

Where was I on December 7, 1941? How could I forget. What a change of mood I had, for I had just left the annual rendition of "Handel's Messiah" that Indiana University (where I was a student), gave before the beginning of the Christmas holiday. Nothing was more spiritually moving to me than the "Messiah." I lived for the "Hallelujah Chorus." The music department at Indiana University would join with the people of the Bloomington, Indiana, community to do the entirety of the great work.

I was jarred emotionally when, after a long walk from the campus, I heard people shouting in the center of town, "Japan has bombed the United States! We are at war!" I was a junior at I.U., and my mind immediately jumped to whether I could finish my work.

When I reached the place where I lived on the west side, Mrs. Duerson, my landlady, was getting the news on the radio. It was a day to live in infamy. It began as an afternoon of joy for me and ended as an evening of apprehension for me and my country. I never dreamed that a small country like Japan would attack a big and great country like the United States.

LAURA BURROW

It was a cold Sunday on December 7, 1941. I was in Fargo, North Dakota, seventeen-years-old, and working as a mother's helper. My girlfriends and I went to a movie on our time off. Coming from the movie around 3 p.m., we heard all this shouting as people gathered on the street. The newspaper boys were holding headlines shouting, "Extra, Extra! Japan attacks Pearl Harbor!" We were all stunned and fearful at what might happen.

I had one brother and naturally thought of him. I later found out he was deferred as my family were farmers. Actually, things became better for the farmers as all farm produce was vitally needed.

Living in a small town, it soon became devoid of young men. Many had put in their years of training and these were the first called. It was hard on some families with more than one boy, and many did not come back. This affected me greatly as I was of that age.

The long-term impact for me was my move to California in 1942 to work in defense. I married my husband, a sailor in the U.S. Navy, which kept me in California. I never have returned to my home in North Dakota.

RUTH HULETT

Yes, I remember hearing the news of the Japanese attack over the radio. It was a clear and sunny afternoon around 3 p.m. It was my father's birthday, and after a family dinner, we were all listening to the radio and discussing current events and politics as usual. We were shocked. It was unbelievable. We were silent until we realized the events, and could not believe how a small country like Japan would dare to attack a big country like the USA. We just looked at each other in shocked silence.

I remember listening to President Roosevelt's announcement the next day. We ultimately felt that Roosevelt saw it coming and let it happen because he needed that war to get the public out of the government payroll and into the factories and war effort. That is what happened.

Ultimately, one of our war generals was blamed for it all in order to pass the buck somewhere else, as we saw it. Not true!

LAUREL M. UDDEN

I was a senior in high school living near Fresno, California. My sister was in nurses' training at Stanford University Hospital in San Francisco. I had gone with my parents that weekend up to San Francisco to visit her.

After going to church that Sunday, we were having dinner at one of my father's relatives, who lived on one of the Twin Peaks of San Francisco. We turned on the radio (T.V. was just getting started in those days) and heard the announcement, "Pearl Harbor has just been attacked, and the planes are headed for San Francisco." It was with mixed feelings that we hurried out of San Francisco, leaving my sister and my father's relative there.

You had to live on the West Coast to understand the immediate hysteria that followed. We had a "brown out" of all advertising lights, billboards, etc. All street stoplights were covered over with a shade much as most of them are today.

My father took turns manning a plane lookout station, much like the forest fire lookout stations. If a plane was spotted, all radio stations would go off the air and we had to turn to KLS in Salt Lake City to find out what happened.

All people of Japanese descent were gathered into camps. One of my best friends was an American-born Japanese, so he was a citizen. But, he had to go with his family into this camp. He was bitter about that, but later joined the U.S. Army and was sent over to Japan after the war as an interpreter. He met his wife in Japan, so it turned out well for him. Before the war, all Japanese students had to study the Japanese language as the parents wanted them to know the language. My friend was not happy about having to go to school on Saturday, but things turned out for the best for him as a result. I still have contact with him and see him from time to time.

Yes, I surely remember December 7, 1941, vividly, as if it just happened.

REVA CLEGG

My husband, Leo Clegg, was out hunting with another friend. We were invited to have dinner with them. My husband and his friend were hunting deer that day, and we gave them the news when they came home.

They were working and helping to build the Anderson Ranch Dam. When their jobs were put on hold, they left. My husband and brother headed back to the mine in Rio Linto, Nevada. Since they had worked there previously, they were picked out of a long line of guys wanting employment. My husband later went to work at the Lark Mine in Utah.

My husband's two brothers eventually had to go to war. My husband was deferred from going to the army because he was the only help his father had on his farm.

JESSIE SLEVITZ

I had taken my mother-in-law to Pennsylvania from Baltimore and stopped in a restaurant to have lunch. Just as we started to eat, the news came on the radio that Pearl Harbor had been bombed. I called home at once and, of course, everyone was upset at this horrible news. I immediately headed for home.

PATRICIA FLOYD

On December 7, 1941, my family and I were returning from a fun day spent in San Francisco. As we approached the San Francisco Bay Bridge, we noticed a teenaged boy holding up a newspaper and shouting, "Extra, extra! Read all about it!" The paper had bold headlines that read "WAR" across the top. We were all in a state of shock.

It was chaos crossing the bridge. Sailors were running to their ships and soldiers to their bases. It was a sight I never will forget.

The war greatly affected our family. My only brother enlisted in the navy and was off to war on a minesweeper. Many of my cousins, all of whom I grew up with, served in the armed forces. We were very thankful that all of them returned home safely.

On the homefront, we were confronted with rationing. Stamps were given out for sugar, butter, and gas. The radio was almost constantly on as it was our communication with the world events taking place.

We lived in the country at the time so there weren't many people to talk to. Our neighbors usually knew about the same information as our family at about the same time.

Anita Andres

I was a junior in high school in Orland, California, when the Japanese bombed Pearl Harbor. It was a Sunday and we had been to church. The 7th of December in 1941 was still in the Depression era. We were like many in our community, poor with few amenities. We had a radio, but never listened to it until the evening news broadcast. For some reason, we had not bought a newspaper that Sunday and therefore were not aware of the bombing for several hours.

I don't remember much about the event, but I do remember the horror of our family and friends as we discussed it. Daddy was a veteran of World War I and extremely patriotic, as were many people at that time. He was sure that if we should enter the war, there was no doubt that "our boys would have an end to it in a matter of weeks." Well, of course, he was wrong about that.

As time went on, we began to hear about the terrible battles and horrible losses by our nation. At first it was like a game. Everyone was laughing and no one seemed to be worrying. The kids at school took it in stride, talking about it freely. The boys were talking of quitting school to join up. If they were seniors and graduating in the spring, then boys that did sign up were promised a diploma just as if they had graduated. They would put those "Japs" in their place.

My brother wouldn't graduate until 1944, but as soon as he was nearing that date, he too signed up. By that time, things were pretty bad over in the Pacific theater of operations. It was bad in Europe too, but it seemed we worried more about the Pacific.

I remember how we had airplane watches. The women and older men would take turns at the station watching for planes overhead and calling in to a headquarters, wherever that might be, giving the approximate altitude of any plane that came into sight. I took my turn at the phone too, although I'm sure none of us knew how high they really were.

As soon as I graduated from high school, I went to work in Sacramento doing my part for the war effort. I worked for the Induction Center for northern California where our young men came for physicals and to be enrolled. It is interesting to note that our work center was in the Japanese Temple in Sacramento. That area of the city was predominantly Japanese and they had been evacuated to concentration camps. At that time, we thought it only fair that we should use their temple for that purpose. It never occurred to us that we were actually desecrating their holy place. But there were many things that were done in the name of the war effort.

Of course, during these years, we had rationing. We had ration stamps for meat, butter, gasoline, sugar, and even shoes. I have forgotten many of the things we had to have stamps for.

I met several sailors and other military men who made it through Pearl Harbor. They told us of the terrible bombings and atrocities that had happened. But I was not personally involved with any of these events. I did have a close friend, a girl, who worked with me, and was from Hawaii. She had some interesting things to say, but most of the incidents were hearsay from others.

There was one incident that happened in our town. One day about six Japanese planes came flying low over the buttes west of town. Everyone thought we were going to be bombed. I think they sped back west again before we knew what was happening. It did create a big concern.

Selwyn Hirsch

On December 7, 1941, I was at Carnegie Hall in New York City at a concert of the New York Philharmonic Orchestra. About halfway through the concert, a man came out of the wings and stopped the music and announced that the Japanese had bombed Pearl Harbor. I believe he also said President Roosevelt had asked Congress for an immediate declaration of war.

There was a stunned silence until broken when the orchestra began to play "The Star-Spangled Banner." The entire audience stood and sang the anthem with such fervor as I have never heard since. It was just like a scene from the movies. I remember thinking that the world would never be the same again. Of course it wasn't.

The company I worked with used a lot of brass and nickel silver, materials which became frozen by the government. I decided to go to California and work in the aircraft industry. As a result, I was able to make a major career change which affected my whole future. In California, I also met my future wife, and this also greatly affected my life.

THOMAS P. FARBO

I clearly remember that Sunday in early December. I was in my hometown of Windber, Pennsylvania, a small coal mining company town seven miles south of Johnstown, Pennsylvania.

The day was crisp but clear, and the sun was bright—almost shimmering. I was sixteen-years-old and on my way home from attending church (a short three-quarters of a mile hike). I stopped at our neighborhood hangout, Dippy Cannoni's grocery store on 21st Street. The small, two-room store also accommodated a noisy but ruly group of boys (about fifteen) that drank sodas, played the pinball machines, and discussed and cussed over all current sports and the stars—DiMaggio, Ted Williams, Akry Vaughn, Ducky Medwick, Babe Ruth, etc.

I stopped at Dippy's and was amazed that only two of us occupied the store. I recall buying a cream soda and playing the pinball machine. The radio was on and I think soft music was playing. The time was about 11 a.m.

That Sunday, no one entered the store. Dippy and I exchanged comments on the president's imminent declaration of war, not really absorbing the significance of this event, and how the lives of many people in Windber would be immediately and forever affected. Many would never see home again.

I quickly ran the short distance home and blurted out the news to my mom, sister, and four brothers—all younger than myself. My mom was upset and verbally chewed out the American as well as the Japanese governments. She could see her sons going off to war, especially her oldest boy—me. I felt I was always her "pet." My sister, nine months older than I, was enthralled—soldiers, sailors, celebrations. She saw a different picture of the announcement of December 7, 1941.

The peace and quiet of the following morning was broken by a special announcement that "the President of the United States was going to speak." President Roosevelt spoke about "the dastardly attack by the Japanese Empire on our naval base at Pearl Harbor killing many Americans and causing major damage to the Pacific Fleet and military installations."

After the news, the family retired to its routine of chores, school, and a visit with grandma and grandpa as well as my four uncles and aunts (dad's side). The war news, three doors away at my grandparent's, erupted into a volcano of emotion, fear, and constant turmoil about our young men going to war and the possibility of them getting killed. Being Italian Americans, their concern, love, and respect for America overpowered their fears of losing loved ones. These people were the true heroes of the many days that followed December 7, 1941. We would have never won the most recent "war to end all wars" without them and their children.

WILDA PEARSON

As far as information on World War II goes, I don't have much. I do remember, however, where I was when Pearl Harbor was bombed. I was in Muncie, Indiana, at a bowling tournament when someone said we were at war. We all gathered around the radio as we couldn't believe it. Sure enough, we were.

I worked at a defense plant here during the war. Lots of men and boys I knew had to go. Some from here never made it back.

MERIE BROWN

It was a beautiful winter's day, sunny, but crisp in Seattle, Washington, on December 7, 1941. I had the day off from "Ma Bell," as we called the telephone company. We had planned a nice day with a bunch of young people looking for fun at the home of a boy friend's parents.

Someone turned the radio on and the whole world stopped. The Japanese had bombed Pearl Harbor! Pearl Harbor, such a faraway world. Why should that affect us?

The next day, December 8, my twentieth birthday, I returned to work. I entered the telephone building and showed the guard my I.D. with my picture as usual. Today, in addition, I signed my name in or out of the building. I also opened my purse and packages for inspection. There were many, many new rules and regulations.

I proceeded up in the elevator to the long distance and information floor. It was a madhouse! I sat on my high stool at the position assigned me, put on my earphones and mouthpiece, plugged into the socket, and the madness began.

The thousands of tiny lights from the wallboards around the room were so bright they actually hurt my eyes. No matter how hard I, along with about 120 other girls tried, we couldn't answer all of the calls. Each light I answered was from a frantic person trying to reach a friend, relative, or loved one.

No ship-to-shore or overseas calls were being accepted. Most circuits were busy. Very few calls could be completed.

That day I realized how close Pearl Harbor had become. I left my teen years behind and entered the world of adults. I had become just a tiny part of the war effort.

D. MANCHESTER

I do remember December 7, 1941. I lived in upstate New York. I don't recall what kind of day it was, only it must have been cold. We always had our Sunday dinner about one o'clock. We finished our meal and started to clean up when someone turned on the radio. Well, everything stopped when we heard the news.

It had a big impact on us as it did all Americans. We had young men in the family and they knew they would be going to fight. It was indeed a very sad day. I had two brothers in the service—one in England and one in Germany. There were many cousins and friends involved also. I only wish there would never be another war anywhere.

ROSEMARY ANDRES

The following was written by me on December 9, 1941:

Two days ago on December 7, the Japanese nation made an unprovoked and dastardly attack on the Hawaiian Islands. Not only was it unprovoked, but it came entirely as a surprise to both the islands and the United States because, at the time, the Japanese envoy was, and is, in Washington, DC to confer with the American president, President Franklin D. Roosevelt. They were trying to negotiate peace terms on which both the Japanese and United States would agree. It is hard to believe we are now in war.

It is true the Eastern Hemisphere has been fighting for well into two years, but that was practically another world away. Now we must run for shelter whenever we hear a plane overhead. Now we must be content with having our radios suddenly go dead because there is a raid over that city. Now we must be saddened by news that someone we knew has been killed in action or had a son who was. Now, in other words, things have changed.

I once thought that I didn't live in an exciting era, but I have changed my mind completely now. I wonder where it all will end. What will my thoughts be as I read this at some distant future date? Will I be there to read it? That is a question that only time can answer. I cannot believe that democracy will fail, but Rome, with all its glory, faded and died. I shall hope and pray for the best anyhow.

DOROTHY BEAUDETTE

On the 6th of December in 1941, it snowed. The 7th proved to be a bitterly cold, cloudy, and windy day. We were in a farm home in Rosalie, Nebraska, having lunch with Marlow and Gladys Tipton. We had the radio on and heard that Pearl Harbor had been bombed. We were all very sad and angry to think this could happen. We knew that it would take our brother and brother-in-law off to fight.

Another guest was John Tipton who had stood up with us at our wedding. He said, "I'm on my way to Omaha to enlist." He joined the air force and became a squadron leader testing planes. He was later killed testing a fighter plane. He told his commander the plane wouldn't do what they wanted it to do. The young man who came home with his body said it was the only time "Tip" had pulled rank and flown the plane himself. He was making a high dive and the wings tore off the plane. He went straight into the ground. It was a sad day for us all.

My brother, Burdette Lorenzen, was in Italy part of the time. One of his jobs was to go behind lines and try to salvage parts of planes to repair the ones in his unit. One of the hard parts was when the war was over, my brother wasn't allowed to come home home right away. He remained in the hospital for awhile.

My brother-in-law, Lloyd Ballard, was in all battles with Japan.

My next door neighbor, Donald Beaudette, was amongst the many who trained in Windover, Utah, with the 590 Compsite Group. His plane, "Straight Flush," was to be the third plane to drop an atomic bomb if needed.

For me, I saved all stories that were written in the newspaper about World War II. In all, our problems at home weren't so hard to take when you consider how tough the boys overseas were having it.

My husband couldn't pass the test to go into the army so he stayed home. We farmed 400 acres at that time, milked cows by hand, and raised hogs. We had a farm tractor but also planted corn with horses. We had no four-row or larger planters then.

December 7th upset us to think we could be caught off guard so. This terrible thing would make families all over the world suffer with the loss of fathers, sons, and brothers. It was a sad day we will all remember.

LOUISE B. BALTIKAUSKI

I lived in Cottonwood, Alabama, at that time while I was teaching school there. I resided at a boardinghouse, and was there on my bed painting my toenails when I heard the terrible news from a radio station out of Dothan, Alabama, on that cool Sunday afternoon.

I remember having feelings of shock and sorrow. Everyone wondered how the sneak attack could have happened. I called my mother and father with the news. That upset them because I had a brother who would be most likely affected. Everyone was in a state of shock and no one even wanted to eat or do any of the usual things. The church was full that Sunday.

CECILIA SVITEK

I'm nearing my eighty-fifth birthday and I remember very well when newsboys were yelling, "Extra, Extra! Read all about it!" on the corner of the streets about the Pearl Harbor attack.

It was Sunday, December 7, 1941. I don't know how early it came on the radio news because it was Sunday. We went to church, prepared dinner, ate, then cleared off the table. My husband then put on the radio. It was about twelve-thirty or one o'clock when we heard it. We were busy cleaning the kitchen but ran into the living room to hear the news.

It was a shock because we had men nearby crippled from previous wars. It sure put a scare to families with young men. My husband had four brothers and a sister going in. Thank God they all came back home.

RUTH BEAVERS

I was living in Nevada at that time, my husband and I. I heard the doings on the radio. That's all we had back then. I thought, "Oh, what is that?" not believing that it was a real broadcast. I couldn't believe that any war would come to the United States. I finally realized that the broadcast was real.

I could hardly wait until my husband got home. He had already heard the news, everybody had heard it. It was something. We just couldn't believe it. It was a real surprise attack. That, of course, changed the whole picture of our lives.

My husband and I had been in Nevada for only three or four years. He had his own business started and was doing very well. He was having a little bit of a problem getting priorities on his materials. He figured that if a war came on, we didn't have a big enough company to get the materials needed for building.

My husband would be thirty-eight on his next birthday, and they weren't taking any married men over thirty-eight. So, he wanted to volunteer—

go in as a private. He figured that if he did that, maybe others would start volunteering. So, we closed the business, gathered our belongings up, and had to get rid of the house we had been paying on. We moved back East so I could live with my parents. We couldn't believe how fast things were moving.

My husband did volunteer and they took him. It almost killed him that a thirty-nine-year-old friend he met up with in the service was sent over to Europe while my husband had to stay home.

At home, I managed to get a job in ladies' ready-to-wear—selling, buying, and modeling.

Edith Friedman

On December 7, 1941, a Sunday at 11 a.m., I was in my kitchen cleaning vegetables for an early Sunday dinner. I had my radio on with music. Suddenly, there was an interruption on the radio. Pearl Harbor had been bombed. I thought it was a program and changed to another station only to find the same announcement.

Of course I didn't believe it, but I awakened my husband anyway. That was the beginning of a nightmare. My husband was inducted several weeks later, as a medic in the air force, until January 1946.

I called my family in New Haven, Connecticut, as I had two brothers in their twenties. Of course this changed our lives forever. December 7, 1941, will always be a day of turmoil and never-forgotten memories.

Shirley Martell Mills

It was a cold day and I was helping my father do some tractor work on the farm out by Clements, California. We noticed there were many more planes flying than usual and wondered about it. We didn't hear about the attack until we arrived home in the late afternoon. It was hard to believe because nothing like that was even suspected.

I didn't have any brothers, but I had cousins that entered the service. We were fortunate that only one was wounded. My boyfriend did not have to serve because he worked with food products that were sent to the troops. We married the next year, and just as the time was getting close that he would eventually be drafted, the war ended.

I remember being parked in front of the Lodi Public Library when the announcement came over the radio that the war was over. I got out of the car and yelled to the passersby that the war was over!!

SAMUEL SILVERMAN

On December 7, 1941, I was age fifteen. That Sunday, my brother, a neighbor, and I were watching the Washington Redskins playing, I believe, the Philadelphia Eagles at Griffith Stadium in Washington, DC, where I was born and raised. The weather was good; the crowd was big and jubilant.

Suddenly on the loudspeaker came the announcement, "All military personnel report to your stations!" We three, and others, did not make much of that, nor did we understand why there was such an announcement. The game continued as before.

When we arrived home later that afternoon, my mother was there to greet us. As was the normal thing to do on most days of the week, especially on Sunday, we put the radio on, or it was already on when we came into the house. It didn't take long to hear the important news that Pearl Harbor had been bombed or attacked.

At the outset, we three (my father had died when I was five-years-old), hearing this announcement, were puzzled because I don't think any of us knew anything about Pearl Harbor. As a matter of fact, I distinctly remember my mother asking or saying, "WHO is Pearl Harbor?"

President Roosevelt, on December 8, went to Congress and announced during his "infamy" speech that the United States was now in a state of war with Japan. Then, gradually, the country began its activities for war. Men and women went off into the various services—some never to return. I believe ten million were in uniform for the U.S.A. at the war's height. My two brothers went; later I went to serve.

My mother and step-father displayed the three-star service flag in one of the front windows. Shortages and rationing were gradually felt with tires, gasoline, flour, sugar, cars (many new ones weren't made for three to four years), some clothing, meat, etc. There were air-raid wardens, sirens, and shelters, some of which were not inhabitable, in case of an attack, like the underground in London. There were blackouts in some cities on the coast at night. The unemployment rate plummeted because of the need for men and women in the service, defense plants, and shipyards throughout the nation.

The greatest impact of a reverse nature was that the continuous forty-eight states were not touched physically by war, at least not the bombing, destruction, or death as it was in Europe, etc. This was a very big and thankful phenomenon.

MAIDA KELLEY

I graduated from Palo Verde High School in Blythe, California, in June of 1941. I was able to get a job at Sprouse Reitz variety store. I was excited to be earning $0.25 an hour. The stores were all closed on Sunday, so I worked forty-eight hours a week and earned $12 a week.

It was about 6:30 a.m. on December 7, 1941, when I got a call that the store was on fire. There was a small independent store next door where the fire began, under suspicious circumstances.

Now I had no job. What was I to do? Quickly I decided to go to San Diego to visit my brother who, after graduating in June, had gone there to work. I boarded a Greyhound Bus with my ticket to San Diego at noon.

At every stop, sailors got on the bus. Finally I heard all their leaves had been canceled because the Japs had bombed Pearl Harbor.

There were forty-five people who graduated in my class of 1941 at Blythe. Twenty-one of them were boys. Most of them went to war. Seven of the boys were killed. Our class president died on the *Arizona* on December 7, 1941.

I truly believe that everyone under the age of fifty should see the movie *Saving Private Ryan* and know that war is very bad and life is short. "Speak softly and carry a big stick" should be the motto of the U.S. government.

MERRILL BRIGGS

My husband was working at Great Lakes Steel in Ecorse, Michigan. Work was slow in the mills so he was only working two days a week. Another friend, also working two days, asked, "Why don't you rent half of our house? That would make it easier for both of us."

We had a very large bedroom for living and sleeping, and a dinette room for eating. They had the dining room. They had a five-year-old girl and we had a one-year-old boy. Since the four of us, myself, husband Ray, Hilliard and Viril Tomlinson, liked to play cards, we played a lot. That Sunday, we fixed dinner to have together. When everything was in the oven and the dessert in the freezer, we played cards all day and evening, except for eating and taking care of the children.

No one turned the radio on. At ten o'clock, Hilliard suddenly remembered the paper which was still on the porch. He called to us in a very excited tone of voice. He said, "War! War! We are at war!"

I must say that work improved rapidly and the cards stayed in the drawer.

RAY SCHOTT

It must have been around 11:30 a.m. Pacific Standard Time since I had just driven home from Sunday school in my Model A roadster. I was walking towards the house when our neighbor, Mrs. Williams, called over in an excited manner, "Did you hear that Pearl Harbor has been bombed and that several American ships have been sunk?"

I called my mother and she came out to hear the news while I went in the house and switched on the news for the latest reports. The accounts were skimpy and more-or-less repetitious. I think for the rest of the day, 90 percent of Americans were glued to their radio sets.

Burbank, California, of course, being home to Lockheed, builders of the Hudson bomber and P-38 fighter planes, would be a logical target in case of any attack on the West Coast.

That evening we experienced our first blackout. Everyone was on edge. I drove, with no headlights, with a couple of buddies, up the hill where we could view the whole San Fernando Valley. The sirens were sounding and all of the streetlights were off. House lights were going on and off sporadically. It was really weird.

From our vantage point on the hill, we could see searchlights from down around Long Beach and Los Angeles to the south, and out towards Santa Monica to the west.

It may have been our imagination, but we thought we heard planes overhead. The army must have been edgy too because we could see tracer bullets firing from the direction of the harbor.

Rumors were flying as fast as those tracers. "They had bombed Long Beach!" and "A submarine had landed in Santa Monica!" could be heard. Almost immediately, suspicion arose about the loyalty of our fellow citizens—the Japanese Americans.

All proved to be false, but it was a day that would change all of our lives and begin four years of war. This day of infamy would forever remain frozen in the minds of an entire generation.

5
ANSWERING THE CALL

In 1941, there were 1,800,000 personnel on active duty in the United States military,[1] and 14,000,000 men aged twenty-one to thirty-five eligible for Selective Service classification.[2] The latter doubled in 1942 when the classification was expanded to include those in the age range of eighteen to thirty-seven.[3] War was in the air in 1941, and most men of draft age were well aware of that fact.

In Europe, the Germans had committed more than three million men to a 1941 attack on the Soviet Union. Politics and the lack of cohesive intelligence reports proved to be the only impediments keeping Hitler from bringing the war in Europe to a swift conclusion.[4]

In the Pacific, Japan had a military push under way for several years in China. In the summer of 1940, however, Japan put the China offensive in a holding pattern and concentrated its efforts in obtaining raw materials for their operation from the many foreign-controlled Pacific Islands.[5] These materials were deemed essential to Japan's war effort and self-sufficiency. This put Japan's relationship with Great Britain at risk.

In the summer of 1941, Japan began its occupation of many of those islands, including parts of Indonesia. The United States responded by freezing Japanese assets under U.S. control. An embargo was also placed on oil destined for Japan.[6]

By the time talks between the United States and Japan began to break down, the notion of war against the United States and Great Britain had already been mentioned by the Imperial Conference, the British constitutional conferences of 1926 and 1930 that dealt with a unified stance against any aggressors, yet retaining the ability to remain as autonomous communities within the British Empire.

The diplomatic demands put in place by the United States were far too great for the empire of Japan to accept. Therefore, the Japanese government saw no reason to continue a diplomatic solution and turned its attention toward war. If a military strike did not cripple the United States, it might buy Japan enough time to settle the conflict in the South Pacific before any foreign powers had the chance to intervene.

Chapters 5 and 6, "Answering the Call" and "Serving Proudly," contain accounts by men who either went into the service as a result of the Japanese attack, or those who were already serving their country in December 1941.

BILL CHASE

I am a seventy-four-year-old combat infantry disabled veteran. I still have a bullet in my throat to prove it.

Yes, I recall vividly December 7, 1941, and I cry. I was sixteen-years-old and working as an usher in what was, at that time, a very impressive and ornate movie theater. It was in the Bronx, New York, on the Grand Concourse, called Lowes Paradise Theater. During the movie, I was standing at my post in the rear of the theater when the film stopped and the theater lights came on.

Jerry DeRosa, the theater manager, went to a microphone at stage center accompanied by two military policemen. One was a GI and the other one was a shore patrol. DeRosa read from a paper he held in his hand. It may have been a telegram from Washington, DC. He announced that the Japanese had bombed Pearl Harbor that morning and that all military leaves had been cancelled. All personnel were to report to their respective headquarters immediately.

I also clearly recall the overall air and attitude of the audience (Thousands of people. It was the largest theater in New York City). I remember the serious looks on the servicemen's faces as they stood up and put on their uniform jackets, unfastened their caps from their epaulets and placed them on their heads, and buckling their belts as they slid out of their seats and walked down the aisle towards the door. It was a very serious episode, and no one was joking or asking for a refund. Very little was said as the audience departed.

I returned to school, joined the National Guard, and subsequently entered the army. I ended up being part of the D-Day invasion during the European campaign.

After the war, I became a federal agent and retired after thirty years. I then became a private investigator and have been prosecuting criminals for the past twenty-one years. I have led an exciting and colorful life.

December 7, 1941, still looms large in my memory. I frequently recall the sober response and dutiful attitude of my fellow Americans that day, some of whom never returned. I am proud.

FRANK GIORDANO

At that time, my age was fifteen-years-old. I was a newspaper boy for *The Boston Daily Record* that was sold in Providence, Rhode Island.

December 7, 1941, is a day I have never forgotten. I am now seventy-two-years-old and served in World War II and the Korean War. The news came over the local radio station while I was getting ready to go to work selling papers.

My family was shocked and angry about the attack on Pearl Harbor. My older brother, Vincent, joined in January 1942, and when I turned seventeen-years-old, I also enlisted in the navy. My brother and I never saw each other from 1942 until 1946, when I came home.

I was proud to serve my country and still am. I belong to Primmer/Cordiero VFW Post 5385 where I am Past Post Commander/Sr. Vice Commander. I am now filling in as Jr. Vice Commander.

The attack on Pearl Harbor was a blow to us. But in the end, we, the people of the United States of America, responded in a way that the Japanese will never forget. We must always be on alert so that there will never be another Pearl Harbor. We must remain strong for the defense of our country and others around the world.

DON OLIVER

I remember well the news of Pearl Harbor. We were at home that day eating and listening to the radio. The announcer's voice came on. He told us about the attack of the Japanese on Pearl Harbor. We heard it all with disbelief. But enough of that, we were on our way to the war.

We were sent to Camp Elliot near San Diego in California. There were a lot of sailors there from all over. It was a tent camp for we who were waiting for a ship. A tent camp was one that had wood floors and sides. The canvas top let in wind and dust from the desert where Camp Elliot was located. Not too comfortable, but not too bad if you were there only a few days, which we were. A few days didn't mean much to a bunch of young sailors who were waiting for a ship. We were just out of boot camp and looking for a new adventure. Sure enough, it began.

After a few days, the officer in charge came in and told us to pack our gear and be ready to leave. About 10 p.m., a big truck came, we loaded up, and took off for our ship.

It was about midnight when we got there. It was a small destroyer called the *Livermore*. It didn't look too big alongside of a battleship and a cruiser. But the bunch of us, about thirty men, became part of a crew of about 300 men. It was mostly confusion. Those in charge didn't know what to do with us.

They sent us down below and told us to find a place to sleep until they could assign us a bunk. Now, down below was the mess hall of our ship. We went to sleep on the tables, decks, and foot lockers.

The ship left port that night. We were at sea when we woke up. That day they told us what our station was and found a place for us. Our career as sailors began. We were on our way to Pearl Harbor to see for ourselves what the Japanese had done.

Characters! We were all characters in those days—320 aboard one ship!

DELBERT LE DOUX

When Pearl Harbor was attacked by the Japanese on December 7, 1941, I was running a truck line that I owned at Brainerd in Minnesota. I heard the reports of the bombing the next day on the radio because there was no television in those days.

My first response was that I would have to get someone to take over my truck line because I knew that I would be in the armed forces before long. In my trucking work, I was contracting with the railroad to haul freight.

I was twenty-nine-years-old at the time, married, and had two children, a son and a daughter. Even though I had a family to support, I knew that I would be called upon for service. The federal government started calling up men right away after war was declared against Japan.

I went up for deferment. I wanted to be deferred for about three months so I could hire someone to take care of my truck operation, but they wouldn't give it to me.

Some of my friends from the Brainerd area in Minnesota were killed in the bombing at Pearl Harbor on that fatal day. I went into the United States Army on January 1, 1942, and served in both the European and Pacific theaters of operation. I received my discharge in December 1945.

EDWARD T. RICHARDSON

I was a twenty-year-old sophomore in Bowdoin College, Brunswick, Maine—an old, small liberal arts college. It was a Sunday afternoon, and as was my custom, I took a break from studies to listen to the New York Symphony concert on the radio. When I turned the switch, there was no concert but the solemn voice of H. V. Kaltenborn, a well known commentator of the day, giving some of the first sketchy reports of the attack.

That evening I was the dinner guest of Len, my freshman roommate, at the Chi Psi Lodge, his fraternity. I arrived at dinner time to find him arriving from the movies. These Sunday evening candlelight dinners were a regular part of the intrafraternity social life at that time. The first thing I asked him was what he thought of the news. He knew nothing about it. When I told him, his first question was, "Where and what is Pearl Harbor?" I told him, having just learned that myself. His next remark was, "Why, they can't do that. That belongs to us."

I think his ignorance and attitude were typical, not only of the students, but of people in general around here at the time. We had turned our backs on the war (in Europe) thinking it of little concern to us. Well, in the flickering candlelight of that evening, we began to feel our ivory tower starting to crumble. The room was heavy with "bad vibes."

I went on to graduate, then into the army for three years—seven months of that was spent in infantry combat in Europe in the 9th Infantry Division. Luck rode my shoulder and I came out with no serious injury. I later went to law school on the GI Bill, then on to a satisfying thirty-year practice.

Arthur Hechinger

I was seventeen years of age and still in high school. On that infamous day in 1941, I was playing a game of pool in the local billiard hall. About 3 p.m. that afternoon, everybody in the place heard of the attack. My first reaction was, "Where is Pearl Harbor?" We didn't, and couldn't, grasp the depth of what was taking place at that moment.

That following year when I finished high school, 1942, I enlisted in the U.S. Air Corps, as it was then called. I did my basic training at Atlantic City, then was sent to Tyndall Field, Florida, to Aerial Gunnery School where I earned my wings. I spent thirty-eight months in the service. I was discharged December 1945.

Richard Frock

In 1941, I was sixteen-years-old and lived with my parents in the small town of Walnut Creek, California, which is about fifteen miles east of Berkeley. My father was an inspector in the Berkeley Police Department. Two of our closest family friends, Jack Mann, a sergeant in the department, and his wife, Edna, lived across the street from the police department.

On December 7th of that year, I drove my mother into Berkeley in my 1929 Franklin, to the Mann's to pick up the lumber they had for us. Jack Mann was a radio buff and had a shortwave radio. While we were there, we heard of the bombing on his radio.

I must admit, I wasn't sure where Pearl Harbor was. I had heard of it and knew it was in the Pacific, but didn't know exactly where. Jack knew and told me of the importance of it as a naval base. Of course, as the news developed during the day, we became more and more aware that war was imminent.

My mother was, of course, concerned because of my age, and my father immediately began checking to see which branch of the service would give him the most favorable position. He had been a buck sergeant in the Marine Corps during peacetime and they offered him his old rank back—after boot camp of course! The Coast Guard offered him the position of chief warrant officer, which he accepted. He arranged for me to attend the Coast Guard Academy upon graduation from high school (after passing the entrance exams).

But, I suddenly learned I was much smarter than my father. Instead of spending the war in school in Connecticut and graduating in three years (accelerated course) with a degree in engineering and a commission in the Coast Guard, I chose to enlist in the Marine Corps. I spent the war in the Pacific, contracted pneumonia, severe dysentery, and dengue fever three times. The third time resulted in yellow jaundice as well as having a great many Eastern gentlemen striving to take my scalp. But I went through four campaigns without being wounded. My mother also served. She was in the WACs (Women's Army Corps).

LAWRENCE J. KRAMER

Where was I when the Japanese hit Pearl Harbor? On December 7, 1941, a neighbor and I were duck hunting in northern Holt County, Nebraska. It was too nice of a day for duck hunting, but it was the season so we had to go out and try it. No luck. About 4:30 p.m. we gave up and went home.

When we got home, we were surprised to hear that the Japs had attacked Pearl Harbor. What amazed me was how the Japs could cross the Pacific Ocean and not be detected. It seemed like we just let them attack us so we could declare war against them, which we did. Just what was the Japs' reasoning in attacking, leaving Pearl Harbor in ruins, and just rambling back home? Why didn't they just bypass the islands and hit the West Coast of the USA? We had three bombers in the continental United States and a handful of fighters. The rest of our equipment was over in Europe fighting the Germans. We were just a sitting duck. Thank God they didn't (hit the continent).

How did that affect my family? I'm sure that my mother was devastated. She was afraid that all of her boys would be drafted. As it was, my older brother was a mechanic who was keeping farm machinery running and was excused. My next brother was running my folks' farm and was excused.

I was just a banker with no excuse, so I decided to enlist in the Army Air Corps. I finally wound up as a bombardier on a B-24. We were a ten-man crew. We flew forty-five missions in the South Pacific.

My younger brother was drafted. My youngest brother was too young. I'm sure two out of five was distressful enough.

What is my feeling now? I must have dropped 200 tons of bombs. Our usual target was a Jap-held air strip, but how many natives and how many little shavers did I destroy? How many Japanese, and maybe a few Americans? Just who is responsible for all of the killing?

I pray that God will forgive all of the people responsible for all of the wars this country has been involved in. I hope and pray that mankind will finally wise up and stop being so greedy. If countries like China continue to develop the technology that they stole from us, may God forgive us for developing our own destruction.

W. ERICKSON

On Pearl Harbor Day, I was at the airport. Although the day was clear and visibility good, we had two feet of snow. We were in the process of putting skis on the J2 Cub when Kenny Tjernlund drove up with his radiator steaming. He said that the Japs had attacked some place called Pearl Harbor. Some of the group didn't know where it was.

The owner of the plane, Lawrence Olson, wanted to put the plane back in the hangar. I said, "No, let's fly around the patch once. We did, and he let me go around once in the two-seater. I said that our world, with the Depression, would never be the same again.

It wasn't. The next day, the CAA grounded everyone and required all airplanes to be guarded or disassembled. Ole went into the glider troops. He got by without a scratch, but his letters were like Technicolor. Not long after his return, he got a strange disease and wasted away in a state hospital in Newberry. He had flown four or five invasions in CG4A gliders.

I went into air traffic control and then into the infantry. After a cruise to Saipan, I returned for ten years to my control tower job, this time in Spartanburg, South Carolina.

Pearl Harbor was no surprise to me. I expected it. So did the president, as did General Marshall. They had been warned of the wheres and when. There was no personal aftermath to speak of, until I was in Eniwetok Atoll and they dropped the bomb. I was lucky to have survived.

John R. Joseph

I had already fulfilled my normal Sunday obligation of attending Sunday Mass at St. Joseph's Roman Catholic Church in Mahanoy City, Pennsylvania. My birthplace and hometown was in the center of the anthracite coal (hard coal) region of northeastern Pennsylvania.

On that date, I was single and working as a laborer in a "bootleg" coal mine/hole on one of the hillsides that surrounds our town. I was twenty-years-and-five-months-old, and as was normal in our area at that time, we men who had already fulfilled our Sunday obligation, congregated in the closest poolroom to our homes. We had a hard and fast rule: No women or girls allowed beyond the swinging doors that led to the pool table and card table.

There is a misnomer attached to those institutions. People referred to associates in a poolroom as "loafing in the poolroom." Wrong! Get into the right one with the right guys, and it is like an institution of higher learning. You got a refresher course of what you were taught, learned, and retained at home. You learned how to count, think, play cards, respect and defend the elders, children, and ladies. You learned to temper your language, practice courtesy, and respect the law. Break one of the rules in the poolroom and you got suspended from attending.

I was shooting pool with some of my buddies when the news came over the radio that the Japs had attacked Pearl Harbor in the Hawaiian Islands. I don't recall if the sun was shining that day or not, but the sobering news seemed to draw a curtain across the skies, especially when they gave estimates of how many Americans lost their lives in that sneak attack.

The news infuriated me, especially when we realized that while those Jap bombers were attacking and killing our soldiers and sailors in Pearl Harbor, the Japs had their peace envoys in Washington, DC with an olive branch in their hand.

We did not have to tell anybody about the sneak attack because every radio in our town of 16,000 (then) was tuned to the stations that were broadcasting the news.

Those of us who did not have wives or children to consider, began discussing what branch of service we were thinking about entering. We were looking for revenge for that dastardly deed, especially when we heard the sorrowful news that one of our local boys, aged twenty-three, lost his life on December 7, 1941, at Pearl Harbor.

The Goody Two-shoes of today's modern society consider "revenge" as a nasty word, but Webster's describes revenge as, "To inflict punishment or injury in return for a wrong done." What's nasty about that?

Naturally, the sneak attack was the topic of discussion wherever you went that day. Monday, December 8, I reported to work at the bootleg coal mine/hole but only to tell them, "Today is my last day. I am going to join the Army tomorrow." On Tuesday, December 9th, I took the 6 a.m. bus to our county seat in Pottsville, Pennsylvania, walked to the recruiting office and signed up for the U.S. Army. After signing the papers, the recruiting sergeant said, "You're in the Army Air Corps. Go home and wait for my call as there is not enough barracks space to handle all the enlistees." My call came on December 29, 1941.

In addition to myself, I also had two of my older brothers, an uncle, and a nephew that served in World War II.

BILL ROBERTSON

My memory of Sunday, December 7, 1941 is vague. I remember that my friends and I discussed enlisting. I was seventeen at the time, a senior in high school, and living in the Squirrel Hill area of Pittsburgh, Pennsylvania. My parents wanted me to wait to enter college in the fall of 1942.

I entered Carnegie Tech. My dad had heard of a course in Meteorology that was designed for those entering the army. It was sponsored by the University of Chicago. He went to Chicago and acquired details and the method to enroll.

I took voluntary induction and was sworn in on January 11, 1943. I entered the program, attended a service school at Bowdoin College in Brunswick, Maine, and completed the course on February 12, 1944. Since the meteorology course had been canceled, I was assigned to the U.S. Army Air Corps and sent to Selman Field in Monroe, Louisiana for navigation training.

I graduated from this school as a second lieutenant on January 26, 1945. I served as an instructor for a while after graduation, and was then sent overseas on April 6, 1945 where I served until December 15, 1945. My unit was the 46th Troop Carrier Wing, Squadron 317. Our locations varied from New Guinea, Western Pacific, Southern Philippines, Luzon, Okinawa, and Korea. My duties included navigation of C-47s. I separated from the service on April 4, 1946.

LEE R. PHILLIPS

The attack on Pearl Harbor was a big letdown for me and my family. I had just left the Wilder Theater and walked across the street to Taylor's Service Station. My friend, Lem Maxwell, told me he had just learned about the attack on Pearl Harbor.

At that time, I was farming with Mr. Huff and he got me a deferment. But seeing my friends going into the service prompted me to quit farming and I was soon drafted.

I didn't see Pearl Harbor but we went close by it. I was onboard ship for twenty-three days and nights. We landed at Leyte in the Philippines. I was assigned to the 24th Infantry Division and soon went on an LCI boat to Davao, Mindanao. I was stationed in an outpost above Davao when they dropped the atomic bombs on Hiroshima and Nagasaki, Japan. We soon occupied Japan, so despite the opinion of a VA officer, I'm an atomic veteran.

I was awarded the Combat Infantry Badge when I was in the jungle above Davao and was in the rubble of Hiroshima and Nagasaki. The 24th Infantry Division was the first and last to fight the Japanese.

BOB FOLEY

Until 1942, I was able to get two deferments to stay out of the army by hauling aircraft engines from Cartersville, Georgia, to Wright-Patterson Air Force Base (in Dayton, Ohio). I had been driving a truck back from Georgia when I heard the news on the radio while stopping at a gas station.

The first thing I thought was that I was going to be drafted. Following the bombing, I did get drafted. I was in the 94th Medical Gas Treatment Battalion, Company C, dealing with gas, chemicals, and chemical warfare from 1943 until 1945.

Members from Company C still meet for a reunion every year in the fall.

PHILIP MATTHEWS

I remember vividly to this day the Japanese attack at Pearl Harbor on December 7, 1941. I was a sixteen-year-old high school junior in Park River, North Dakota, when our school principal, W. E. Koenker, called a general assembly of all students to hear the president of the United States deliver a speech before Congress. It became the memorable "A Date of Infamy" speech of President Franklin Delano Roosevelt. It was a short, six-minute dramatic message delivered over the radio on Monday, December 8, 1941.

"Yesterday, December 7, 1941, a date which will live in infamy," the president began. "The United States . . . was suddenly and deliberately attacked by naval and air forces of the empire of Japan." President Roosevelt asked Congress for a declaration of war against Japan.

The short speech was drafted by Roosevelt himself. While he was preparing to go to Congress, Roosevelt added the latest battle-related news as it came in, I learned in later years. Harry Hopkins, the special assistant to President Roosevelt, suggested an additional sentence which Roosevelt approved, that expressed confidence that "we would gain the inevitable triumph—so help us God."

I also learned later that the word "infamy" was added to the speech by Roosevelt in an early draft, but the change made the whole phrase of "a date which will live in infamy" memorable. It became memorable even to us as high school students, who had to go to the dictionary to look up the meaning of "infamy."

Little did we know then that many of us, even some of the girls in the audience, would be called upon to fight in the devastating conflict of World War II. I served in the United States Army in France and Germany in 1944, 1945, and 1946.

Lt. M.J. Pulver, USNR Ret.

On Pearl Harbor day, we college kids were lolling around, taking it easy after a night of dancing and fun at this (still) all-male college, Wabash, in Crawfordsville, Indiana. Our dates, all imported from nearby colleges, had left their well-chaperoned housing to come over for breakfast. One of our guys rushed in to announce that "the dirty Japs bombed our base at Pearl Harbor!"

I remember turning to my date (damned if I remember who) and saying dramatically, "Who knows when we will ever dance together again?"

In a sense, it was a relief. Ever since we started school in 1939, there was a war going on and very few figured we wouldn't someday be in it. The navy, Air Corps, and army had been wooing us college boys with special programs for some time, but few took it all that seriously. Now, suddenly I was scrounging through the literature with real purpose.

My parents called, fearful that their only child would soon be cannon fodder. Having served in World War I, dad knew it wasn't all that much fun.

Ah, but the trick was to get your duty lined up while there was still a choice. Wearing glasses meant no air force for me. Then, one of my pals offered me a ride to Chicago. So, on January 11, 1942, I found myself being sworn into the naval reserve. It was their V7 program which called for you to stay in school until your class was called up. That made for some serious nail biting until they got around to me and the five others who enlisted with me over a year later.

Once the navy made up its mind, things went fast. Four months later, Columbia University turned me out as (the original) Ensign Pulver. Sixty days later, I was aboard the USS *Mayrant*, destroyer 402, where for almost three years, I sailed the Atlantic, Pacific, and Caribbean theaters in faithful, if nonheroic service.

And that's how I remember Pearl Harbor.

FRANK GEPPERT

On Sunday morning, December 7, 1941, my parents and I had been to St. Elizabeth's Church in East St. Louis, Illinois. After church, we were going to visit my sister and family in Chester, Illinois, about fifty miles south. We stopped at a Shell station in Belleville at 20th and Main St. for gas. The attendant had his radio on and we could hear it. A flash came across that the Japanese had bombed Pearl Harbor. We turned our car radio on and listened to the bulletins all the way to Chester.

I ended up enlisting in the Army Air Force in October, 1942. I opted for Kelly Field, Texas, and was sent there for basic training and later assignment. In January 1943, I applied for radio school. I was sent to Truax Field in Madison, Wisconsin, and subsequently to Rosencrans Field at St. Joseph, Missouri, for flight crew school. After several other assignments, bases, and schools, I spent the rest of my enlistment in the Alaskan division of the Air Transport Command.

I returned to the states in September 1945. I was sent home on orders for forty-five days, then discharged on the 15th of December, 1945. I returned to my original job and stayed there until 1951.

CLARABELLA COUGHLIN

On December 7, 1941, I was playing bridge in La Jolla, California. My husband, Kerry Coughlin, was employed as a navigator by Consolidated Aircraft of San Diego where the famous PBYs, or Patrol Bombers were built. The "Y" was designated to the Consolidated Aircraft Corporation, as the letter "C" was already given to the Curtiss class.

Some of these planes had been sold to the Dutch government and were being ferried to the Dutch East Indies. They flew from San Diego to Honolulu, then on to Midway, Wake, Guam, and what is now Indonesia. Three of these PBYs set out from Honolulu on December 6. My husband was on one of them. They flew to Midway and stayed overnight, then set out for Wake the following morning.

That fateful day I was playing bridge with some of the wives of the other airmen. When the news of the Japanese attack was broadcast, we sat there stunned. Where were our husbands? They could have been anywhere out there in that vast ocean. We hurried home to wait for news.

Meanwhile, the three planes were called back and notified of the attack on Pearl Harbor. The navy base on Midway was in shock. The three PBYs were commandeered and the airmen waited for orders.

That night, the Japanese shelled the island and did considerable damage, but the Consolidated airmen were not injured. In the morning, one of the navy pilots asked Kerry to take off with him, ostensibly to search for ships to bomb, but actually they soon headed for Honolulu.

All of those airmen came home and formed the nucleus of what became Consairway, an airline chartered by the U.S. Air Corps to fly men and materials into the Pacific war zone, and bring back the wounded and mail. This airline operated until the Japanese surrendered. My husband was chief navigator of this airline which operated out of Travis Air Force Base in Fairfield, California.

Howard Lee

My wife and I were married August 10, 1940. Employment opportunities were not very good here in west central Indiana at that time, so we migrated to the Chicago area.

I took a job working for the American Can Company in Maywood, which is a suburb of Chicago. We lived a lonely life, as we were not used to the big city ways.

December 7, 1941, was a cloudy, cold, dreary day. I was not working on that Sunday. It was about noon when the man who lived downstairs called and said, "Hey Lee, turn your radio on. The Japs have bombed Pearl Harbor."

It had not been too long since Orson Welles had put on a radio program about an army from the planet Mars that invaded New York City. For a while he had his audience believing it was really happening. I laughed and said, "Don't fall for that crap. Orson Welles must be at it again."

It took a while before the awful truth soaked in. A few days later, I took my wife back to her people and took a leave from my job. I was drafted and spent eighteen months in the European theater. That terrible day stands out in my memory as fresh as if it happened yesterday.

Mary Ellen Guay

On December 7, 1941, my dad Remy Ancelin, brother Jean Hartnett Ancelin, and I were heading back to Dallas, Texas after a hunting trip near Kerryville. We had been squirrel and deer hunting in the Texas hill country. My brother and I were riding in the backseat when we heard on the radio that Pearl Harbor had been bombed. I was fifteen and my brother "Bud" was thirteen. We both said that we've got to enlist and help save the country. This reaction was from a couple of teenagers, at that time, too young to even think of fighting in a war.

The adults were stunned. I don't recall their words, but I'm sure that dad, who had been a marine in World War I, thought back to his own wartime service. He served as Pershing's interpreter when they went to France with AEF. He raised us to be patriotic and to respect the flag and military forces of the nation.

As soon as he was old enough, Bud joined the Marines and went to Manchuria. He went back into the Marines two years after World War II and died from wounds received during the invasion of Korea.

I had to wait until I was twenty in 1945 before I could join the United States Navy WAVES. My birthday was three days after Germany surrendered. I was a sophomore at SMU.

I was sworn in on my birthday, May 11, 1945, and went to Hunter College in New York. I had just finished boot camp and had been assigned to Cory Field in Pensacola, Florida, when we dropped the bomb on Hiroshima.

I stayed in the service for a year and met my future husband from New Hampshire, Jim Guay. He served with VP8 21, crew 7 as a navy gunner.

We've been married almost fifty-three years with five children, ten grandchildren, and three great-great grandchildren.

We're very active in the American Legion in Texas.

Don Jurgs

I was still in high school and I remember vividly that I was in my room listening to the Chicago Bears play the Cardinals when the announcement came over the radio. It certainly affected me in that before the war was all over, I had seen infantry combat, was captured by the Germans, and spent fifteen months in a prison camp. It certainly changed the way my life went.

Frederic Viaux

I was living at the American School (Ruston Academy) in Havana as a teacher when I heard the news from another teacher who had heard it on the radio.

This had a particular impact on me because I was to be married on December 12, 1941, in Havana. I first told my future wife who had already heard it. I offered to postpone the wedding. She said, "No, we should go through with the wedding." All of my American friends who were coming to the wedding in Cuba were, due to Pearl Harbor, unable to attend.

The sense was almost one of disbelief, yet we all, Americans and Cubans alike, realized it was true.

Senator Garcia, whose daughter was in my wife's fourth grade class, gave a large cocktail party for us on, I believe, December 8. He became rather high, and when the party was over around midnight, rushed to the Senate chambers, where they were still in session. There, he made an impassioned, arm-waving speech urging the Cubans to declare war on Japan. After the speech, Cuba did declare war on Japan.

The American Embassy came to the school and asked the American teachers to remain in Cuba. The school was right beside a large hotel full of German refugees with whom we were to be friendly. We were given embassy titles. Mine was the junior economic attaché.

I, however, decided to return to the States and joined the navy as a gunnery officer in the amphibious forces.

ZACARIAS CHUA

December 7, 1941, was December 8 in Cebu, Philippines. I was in high school and it was examination day, prior to the Christmas vacation. We were all very happy anticipating Christmas, but hated those exams. I feared very much Oriental history. Those Chinese and Japanese names seemed to be interchangeable and confusing along with their historical dates.

When the news was announced that exams would be canceled and school closed indefinitely because of the Japanese bombing of Pearl Harbor in Hawaii, the whole class was in unison in our jubilation. The first thought that crossed our minds was to see the continuation of the movie series starring Buster Crabbe as Flash Gordon downtown at the Ideal Theatre. We all anticipated exploding traditional firecrackers during Christmas, only this time it was never done because of the war that immediately followed the bombing.

When I came home from school, all our parents, with somber faces, huddled in the middle of the streets, discussing the consequences of the bombing. To us youngsters, it was no big deal. America could simply bomb Japan back—and that's it!

I thought I'd never see, first hand, the brutality of the war. We were involved in the conflict right away when we accidentally met the invading Japanese forces and were slapped in the face several times. Seeing my mother slapped and staggering to the ground jolted me suddenly to manhood. The boyhood innocence left my body as the reality of the war seeped in. I was filled with rage and a desire for revenge. That desire, coupled with patriotism, involved us in the guerrilla movement. Our allegiance to America was demonstrated when our family risked their lives by hiding an American under the noses of the Japanese soldiers during the occupation. My uncle lost an ear when the Japanese soldiers cut it off as the tide of the war turned. I saw before my eyes Japanese soldiers executed by the guerrillas.

I heard the roar, saw the might, felt the power, and smelled the food supplies of the returning American forces. This was followed by brothers killing brothers, as the guerrillas caught up with Filipinos who collaborated with the Japanese.

Now, after these long years, I can still see the jubilation on the face of my granddaughter every time she is told there will be no classes today. Is the next war near?

Bill Helm

I heard the Pearl Harbor news on the radio at home in Elizabethtown, Pennsylvania. I was sixteen at the time, and recall that within two hours, the Lancaster newspaper published a special edition and I was selling newspapers in the town square.

Two of my brothers immediately enlisted—one in the navy and one in the Coast Guard. An older married brother followed.

I left high school midway through my senior year and joined the Coast Guard along with four classmates. My two brothers, who had enlisted first, were both involved in heavy fighting in the South Pacific. This included Guadalcanal, Saipan, Tinian, The Battle of Coral Sea and others.

My older brother was an aircraft mechanic, and was assigned to various naval air stations. I was a kind of tailender, and during the latter stages of the war I was stationed aboard ship on both convoy escort duty and air-sea rescue. I lost a number of friends and several relatives.

Howard Roach

On December 7, 1941, when the Japanese attacked Pearl Harbor, my friend and I were driving around town in downtown Long Beach after church. We had stopped for gas around noon at a station on Ocean Boulevard. I just happened to turn on the car radio and heard the news that Pearl Harbor had been bombed by the Japanese navy.

That afternoon we took a drive over to Terminal Island, which was mainly a large village of mostly Japanese people that worked in the fish canneries. It was almost eerie when we drove down the main street to where the canneries and fishing boats were. There were usually a lot of people on the streets, but on this day the streets were nearly empty.

I was in Poly High School the next day when we heard the declaration of war by President Roosevelt.

Within a couple of months, all of the Japanese that lived in Long Beach and Terminal Island had been relocated to holding camps. Terminal Island was now like a ghost town.

I was sixteen when the war started and decided not to go into the army until I graduated from high school. Another friend and myself decided we would like to go into the Coast Guard or navy. The Coast Guard couldn't guarantee that we could finish our last few months of school before graduation, so we decided to join the navy. They were letting everybody we knew finish high school and graduate.

I was an assistant air-raid warden in our neighborhood for several months prior to going into the navy. I remember the blackouts at night and the dimming of the car headlights.

So up to Los Angeles I went to take my physical, which I barely passed because I was so skinny. I returned to LA on March 9, 1943, to be sworn in. I thought this was going to work out fine because I presumed they would tell me I could finish school. Instead, they told me to be back up there tomorrow morning at 8 a.m. (which was my birthday) to leave for boot camp in San Diego.

Boot camp wasn't so bad except our CPO, L. Zamparini, was an olympic runner. Instead of marching every place, we ran because he could run faster backwards than we could forward.

I was then sent to Aviation Machinist Mate School in Norman, Oklahoma, then on to Corpus Christi, Texas, to Rodd Field. I was made a line chief of twenty-five SNB-2C, which was Squadron 18-C (nickname was Cricket Airlines). Our only claim to fame was that we had Tyrone Power as a cadet.

I stayed at main base until I was discharged December 15, 1945. I was very lucky that I did not have to go overseas. I am still very proud that I was in the navy during the war!

JESS J. AGANEW

I lived in a very small town in Missouri and was a sixteen-year-old junior in high school. I went uptown in the late afternoon when a high school mate named Billy Crossland told me about Japan bombing Pearl Harbor. To be truthful, I didn't even know where Pearl Harbor was. But, as I listened to several people talking about it, and a school friend had just left for the navy, I was very interested in what was going on in the world. I had been reading about Hitler in Europe, and the more I heard, the angrier I got.

The next day I asked my mother if I could quit school and try and join up in the armed services. With her permission, I hitchhiked to Kansas City, stood in a long line, and tried to join the navy. They told me to come back when I was seventeen, so I stayed in school until the next year when I quit and joined up.

On December 8, 1942, I was at Great Lakes Naval Training Station. After twelve weeks of boot camp, I was on my way to the Pacific where I was in eleven major battles before reenlisting for four more years after the war. I was discharged on October 10, 1949.

The war years affected me very much. I grew up overnight and saw and did things I hope no one will ever have to do again.

CLYDE RILEY

The temperature had hovered around zero to four degrees Fahrenheit all morning on December 7, 1941. Shortly after noon, after what had proven to be a harrowing experience, we reached the summit of Mount Mitchell, North Carolina. There was ice everywhere. Long, slender icicles hung from every rock, where water had run. The road up the mountain was unpaved and almost impassable because of the frozen wet dirt. Several times, on hairpin curves, we almost lost the car over the side of the hill and had to jump out of the car and literally push it from the edge.

We thought that was the worst, until we reached the top and sat on blankets to eat our delayed lunch. Someone turned on the radio and we learned of the attack on Pearl Harbor. We sat in silence, stunned at the stark reality. The day that would "live in infamy" had dawned.

"Life will never be the same for any of us," my brother said. This prophetic statement came true. One year from that day, the four of us were in some branch of the military for the duration plus.

The drive back to Blythewood, South Carolina, was somber and silent, for the most part. In a few short weeks, my brother, Jason, was in the air force, a cousin, Kenneth, was in the paratroopers, and Richard, another cousin, was in the army. The last to leave home was the author of this account.

Our parents were amongst those whom we told the awful news of the attack. They were shocked like we were. My dad's face was long and furrowed with care, for he knew his two sons would have to go in the service.

My father had been a lifelong farmer in upper Richland County, just north of Columbia, South Carolina. Our leaving home ended his farming. There was no one to help him work the crops. The operation was reduced to food products for consumption by him and the women folk left at home. Life was truly forever changed for all of us after the attack on Pearl Harbor.

L. FRED VOSSEL SR.

We were on our way to pick up the girls for a double date when all of this came over the radio—Pearl Harbor, etc. After we dropped the girls off, my best friend and myself sat in front of my house and talked about the situation for a while. The next week, we both joined the navy for two years or the duration.

I earned four battle stars and spent four years in two overseas tours. I did see quite a bit of action during World War II as a member of a beach battalion in Sicily and Salerno, as well as on board an LST or Landing Ship Tank, in South France.

I was twenty-five when I got out. I married in 1946 and had two sons. I also joined the inactive reserves in 1947 and got called back in 1950 at age thirty years. I was on active duty for one-and-a-half years. I served as a flight deck corpsman on carriers. I served my country as a volunteer, as have both of my sons.

ROBERT HALL

Two important dates in my memory: December 7, 1941, and the day Kennedy was shot. In 1941, I was Southeast district manager for the Bell and Howell Company working out of Atlanta. On December 7, I was in Virginia (the northern border of my territory) visiting my wife Alice who was teaching at Bridgewater College. It was a beautiful, sunny Sunday and we had dinner away from the college. As we were driving back, we heard the announcement on the radio that the Japanese had attacked Pearl Harbor. There was no one to tell and it was an all-night drive to Atlanta.

My reaction was, "How could they be so dumb."

My schedule was to return to Atlanta. So after leaving Alice at the college, I started south, listening to every radio announcement. Throughout the night there were constant news items quoting just about everybody and reviewing the Japanese representatives in Washington. As I arrived in Atlanta by ten the next morning, I heard the declaration of war as it was broadcast over nationwide radio.

By 1942, I volunteered in the Army Air Corps to become a glider pilot. I spent several months learning to fly at a small airport south of Chicago (Homewood, Illinois). After learning that they already had enough pilots, I was inducted into the army. After basic, I had my choice of schools and went to photographic school at Lowery Field in Denver. I spent the rest of my army time as a photographer in the U.S. Strategic Bombing Survey in both Germany and Japan.

With great interest in motion picture photography (a la B and H), I shot several thousand feet of 16 mm Kodachrome of Japan and spent the next several years as a travelogue lecturer. I was the only one with the Japanese occupation story. Forty years later, I returned to Japan with new film of Hiroshima and lectured on "Hiroshima, Then and Now."

RICHARD RADOCK

I was at home in Fayette County when I heard the news. We had a radio that my dad had built himself. It received station KDKA—the station where I heard the news of the Japanese attack on Pearl Harbor.

I remember it was a cold, overcast day. Most of us were shocked upon hearing the news. As we had the only radio in the area, we relayed the news to all of my relatives living nearby. They knew that something like this might happen, judging by what had been going on in the world.

My brother Joe was in a yearlong training program in the service, and was scheduled to receive time off shortly after the attack. The leave never came. On May 3, 1942, I decided to enlist in the service as all of my gang had gone into the various branches. I tried to enlist in the Marine Corps, navy, and Air Corps but to no avail. I could not pass the eye test because I had to wear glasses. I finally decided I would not wait for the draft. I enlisted July 20, 1942, in the Amphibian Engineers, as a diesel mechanic.

The loneliness we experienced during basic training was overshadowed by the full-time week we devoted to basic. In the evenings we would sit around and relate memorable incidents about our hometowns and families. We lived at the movies and the post exchange during the weekends, sometimes seeing the same movies several times. Reading the hometown newspapers was also a favorite pastime.

After we were properly indoctrinated and received a new series of shots, new clothing, and all of our equipment was crated for overseas, we shipped to Camp Kilmer to get ready for overseas shipment to England. Myself and 14,000 other soldiers debarked on the liner *Queen Mary* on July 3, 1944.

In Europe, we fought through France, Luxembourg, Belgium, Germany, and Austria. There was always a river to cross—sometimes the same river in three places. We saw things that would be burned in the back of our minds forever.

We beat the British across the Rhine by a full day. At that time, they had all of the necessary support, plus several American divisions, to make a big push across. After entering Germany, we received reports of the atrocities that the Nazis had committed.

General Patton ordered every soldier and officer to visit the first death camp at Buchenwald, near Weimar. We trucked in every soldier and checked each one off the roster. At this camp, we saw the ovens and about eighty inmates who were recently shot by the fleeing Nazis. One American paratrooper was among the dead who were piled up like cord wood and covered with lime.

The camp assistant commander was captured in town about to depart for parts unknown. They brought him to see the atrocities; he denied everything and said that he was ordered by Hitler to carry out the massacres. One of the newer inmates pulled a trench knife from one of our soldiers and slit the commander's throat. He then pulled a carbine from another soldier and pumped bullets into his body. The colonel and I were splattered with his blood as we were standing very close. This event was the most gruesome thing I ever witnessed in all of my time overseas. The smell of death can never be forgotten.

We finally left for home from Le Havre, France, around November 17, 1945, and spent five days of our ten-day voyage in a violent storm. As we passed the Statue of Liberty, the sight of that old girl brought to my mind the thoughts I had on the way overseas, which was about a year and a half before.

We landed at Camp Shanks, New York, on November 27, 1945. We were greeted by a general and, after a brief welcome home speech, all of the troops were treated to a steak dinner with all of the trimmings. Then we saw a Broadway show that was in the camp. After two days of physicals and shots, we were shipped to Indiantown Gap, Pennsylvania, for our final mustering out. We were officially discharged from the military on December 8, 1945. It was great to be a civilian again—no more war and no more orders.

6

SERVING PROUDLY

ERNEST WOODALL REAMES

From one of my three wartime journals:

The music on the car radio of the 1927 red automobile was interrupted by an excited male voice. "Ladies and gentlemen, we have been advised that the Japanese have just bombed Pearl Harbor in a surprise attack. All military personnel are requested to return to their bases immediately." The message was repeated and the music resumed.

My buddy, Ike Roeback, continued driving to a place where he could pull off to the side of the road and stop so we could talk about our situation. We were about twenty minutes away from our destination, Walla Walla, Washington, and our dates. This was my second date with Ermalie Shaw, and Ike's was a blind date arranged by my date. Although we were proud of our Army Air Corps insignia, we honored my date's request to wear our civvies instead of our uniforms. Our decision to continue the day as planned was easy, as we decided to return to Pendleton Air Base later that evening.

At the outskirts of town we saw a weathered, crudely lettered sign painted on a two foot by three foot piece of plywood nailed to a fence post. It read, "Soldiers & Blacks not Welcomed." We then realized the reason for our dates' request to wear our civvies.

That sign disturbed me. Eight months had elapsed since my enlistment in the Army Air Corps on May 5th, and I felt a surge of patriotism for my country and disgust for the perpetrators of the sign. My ancestors helped establish American independence in 1777, and a Reames man or woman has been in uniform in all of America's wars and skirmishes since that time. Seeing that sign on the day of America's defeat at Pearl Harbor made me bristle with disgust.

We had been so far removed from the war in Europe, and now on this day, December 7, 1941, we were suddenly thrust into a larger one. I had recently returned from maneuvers with the Russians at Felts Field in Spokane, where several of their pilots were testing out B-25 Mitchell bombers for our country's "Lend Lease" program of war supplies to favored nations. I drove a gas truck and helped keep the planes gassed while on maneuvers. That was as close as I came to war at that time.

This proved to be a life-changing day for me as it was for millions of people worldwide. But for the present time, the few hours ahead were to be enjoyed to their fullest. Tomorrow was another day and would be dealt with later.

We took our dates bowling, then walked through the park to a restaurant where we had a leisurely supper. It was a fun afternoon which climaxed with ice cream and cake at the apartment of Ermalie's uncle and aunt, along with Bert and Rae Shaw who managed the apartment house.

Telling our dates "good night" had a special meaning for Ike and me that evening. The unknown future loomed ahead of us with a forbidding air of uncertainty and apprehension. Our dates also sensed the obscure future that everyone in our country faced, and we promised to write to each other, not knowing where we would be next week. There was no question in our minds about our duty as we returned to Pendleton Air Base before our passes expired.

The next day, December 8th, we heard President Roosevelt on the radio as he gave his famous speech, "a date which will live in infamy." He instilled courage and confidence in all of us early in his presidency with a positive attitude when he stated, "All we have to fear is, fear itself."

Later we were informed about the huge damage at Pearl Harbor, even while the Japanese diplomats talked "peace" in Washington. In less than two hours, eight battleships were sunk or heavily damaged, ten other naval vessels were sunk or heavily damaged, 188 airplanes were destroyed, and 2,396 Americans were lost.

In due time we won the war in Europe and celebrated V-E Day. Shortly thereafter, we celebrated V-J Day with the unconditional surrender of Japan.

Our military commanders, Admiral Kimmel and General Short were later permitted to retire from the military service.

Roy G. Leckner

Having been drafted out of college at age twenty-one, a group of us from Fort Snelling, Minnesota, was sent to Camp Grant, Illinois. This was a first aid, litter-carrying, and therapeutic training location.

There were 180 Americans of Japanese ancestry in for training at the same camp at the same time. We were supposed to be instructors eventually. We drilled with these AJs, played basketball against them, etc. They were hard to understand. Many had some training in Japan.

The morning of December 7, we got cleaned up for church. Most of us were Minnesota Lutherans. We were early for the first service, so we stopped at a barracks close to the church that was all AJs. They were playing poker. One AJ flipped his cards over and reached to turn on the radio. We then heard that Pearl Harbor had been bombed. One by one, the AJs pulled away from the poker table. We went on to church.

The minister talked to us quietly for a while before service started. After we got back to the bivouac area, not an AJ was to be seen. All were at the railroad depot loaded on trains. They were sent to California.

I was later sent to Fort Monmouth, New Jersey, signal school, then on to the South Pacific for four years. My job was to go behind enemy lines and capture Japanese signal equipment for the CIC (intelligence). I came home on a hospital ship.

Leonard Kiesel

I was in the barracks getting ready to fall out for another day of guard duty at the gate of the Jacksonville, Florida, naval air station. We were then ordered to forget about our guard duties and get ready to go out on the waters of Jacksonville's harbor to board and capture three Italian freighters. They were trying to break out into the open sea, perhaps spooked at the news of the Japanese attack on Pearl Harbor. They were ramming the toll bridge that was down, thus keeping them captive within the harbor itself. The orders came from the air station's commanding officer, Captain Mason. He later became a vice admiral in the Pacific War.

While the United States wasn't yet at war with Italy, the declaration was inevitable. Italy made the formal announcement four days later on December 11.

These three freighters were under way at full steam when we climbed aboard the best way we could. That was not very easy to do. We had to climb ropes and cargo nets to board them. None of the Italian crewmen spoke any English so we had to fix bayonets and force our prisoners onto the barge. They converted a barracks into a makeshift jail. The prisoners were still there when I left in February for parachute training.

A formal report was either lost or never filed. Even though denials from the marines and the word "alleged" have surfaced a few times, a few records do exist proving that we were the first offensive action taken by the United States after the attack on Pearl Harbor.

In 1995, the Italian Embassy did send me an archival record confirming that three freighters, the *Confidenza*, the *Ircania*, and the *Villarperosa* had been in Jacksonville, Florida, on or around the date of December 7, 1941, and may have been captured by the United States. Is that not proof enough?

Anyway, I eventually became a sergeant and was sent over to the Pacific. I was wounded on the island of Gavutu during Guadalcanal.

I didn't really give the Jacksonville incident any additional thought until researching my military record. I was surprised to find no mention of the United States's first offensive during World War II in my file. Other military units were being attacked while we were attacking. I don't want a medal. They can keep their medals. I just want to set the record straight. We were the first.

LEWIS WALKER

The date was December 7, 1941. On December 10th, I would have been in the navy one year. I was stationed in Jacksonville, Florida, NAS. My home was in Keokuk, Iowa. I was home on a two-week leave and my dad took me to northern Iowa to see a girlfriend who was going to college there.

On Sunday, December 7th, we were on our way home. It was a beautiful day. As we were going through Cedar Rapids, Iowa, we saw newsboys on the corners holding up papers yelling, "Extra! Extra!" My dad, who was driving, stopped the car and bought a paper. The headline said "Japanese Bomb Pearl Harbor."

We turned on the car radio and heard that everyone in the military should return to their bases right away. I called the navy base as soon as I got home. The officer asked me how much time I had left on my leave. I told him I had a week. He said, "You had better go ahead and take it because it might be the last one you will get for a long time."

ELWOOD CHAMBERS

Sunday morning, December 7, 1941, my wife and I arose early. I was in the navy and had a weekend liberty. We took an early morning bus to Puyallup, Washington, where we would spend the day with relatives.

When we arrived in Puyallup, a loudspeaker was repeating, "All servicemen return to your posts, camps, and ships immediately." I checked with the bus depot and was informed that the next bus to Seattle would be at 1400 hours. We were stuck for the day in Puyallup so we visited with our relatives until bus time. It was here we learned Pearl Harbor had been attacked.

When we started to board the bus for Seattle, the driver said, "Only servicemen are allowed aboard first. If we have room, we'll take others."

I was in civilian clothes. I showed him my pass and we were on our way to Seattle. I took my wife home, changed into my uniform, then headed for Pier 91 where my ship was moored.

As I started down the pier, my ship pulled away from the dock. I then went to the port captain's office and inquired about my ship. I was informed that the destination of my vessel was secret. One would have thought the Japs had landed in Seattle. The Thirteenth Naval District was in a quandary on how to act. After much discussion, the officer of the day told me where my ship could be located. This is how I spent my Pearl Harbor day.

JUSTIN FLOYD

I went into the army in March 1941. The Nebraska National Guard was filling their companies. I took my basic training in Co. F 134 Infantry, then went to the 2nd Battalion HQ in Camp Robinson, Arkansas.

I remember Pearl Harbor like it was yesterday. The day was cloudy and warm. I got a pass to go into Little Rock, Arkansas, about eight miles from Camp Robinson. I ate lunch at the company mess, then caught the bus to Little Rock to see my girlfriend. We got married in 1942 and have been together ever since. There were several girls that stayed at that house. They had heard on the radio about the bombing. It then came on the radio that all army personnel were to report back to camp.

When I returned to camp, there were only soldiers on the streets. All of the civilians were glued to their radios. There wasn't much excitement back at camp. It had been rumored that we were headed for Europe.

I don't know if the news bothered my parents. There was no indication of it in their letters. We had no phone. I didn't see them until June 1944.

The day after Pearl Harbor, we got our orders to go to the West Coast. We loaded all of our vehicles on railroad flatcars. It took us a week to go to Fort Ord, California.

R. H. FLEMING

On December 7, 1941, I was in the forward fire room of the destroyer number 427—*Hilary Pollard Jones* (referred to as the *H. P. Jones*)—two days from Iceland in the North Atlantic Ocean. We were escorting, with other destroyers, the balance of a convoy of seventy-two cargo and supply ships for turnover to British ships. They were responsible to get them to their final designated ports.

We had to protect them from the "Wolf Pack" submarines, day and night sometimes, for up to two weeks. We could never get all of them through the submarines and/or surface "Raiders."

We were told via the ship's intercom system, approximately 10 a.m., that the Japs had bombed Pearl Harbor.

Fifty-seven years later to the day, I wore my World War II cap out and only one man asked where, what, or when about my cap.

VICTOR COX

On December 7, 1941, I had just arrived in Baltimore, Maryland, after a long train ride from Louisiana after 35th Infantry Division maneuvers. My assignment was to attend ordnance school at the Aberdeen Proving Grounds. Upon exiting the train, I was transported to the Proving Grounds immediately and issued a helmet, gas mask, rifle, and full pack, then placed on twenty-four-hour alert along with thousands of other GIs.

I heard the news from the government officials who met us at the train station. Weather wise, I don't recall what kind of day it was, but otherwise I remember it to be a gloomy day with a barracks full of concerned buddies.

It was several days before I received any mail, but when I finally got mail from my wife, mother, and also a couple of sisters, they expressed their concern of what could possibly lay ahead for us all.

I have a twin brother who went into the service at the same time as I did and he was sent across the Pacific. We are grateful that we both arrived safely home.

I might add that I finished the ordnance school, then went by rail to California to join my original company. Under new orders, went back to Aberdeen Proving Grounds for more schooling. From there I was sent to Langley Field, Virginia, as a cadre where we formed a new unit. After much training we went by ship across the Atlantic to the European theater of operations. The rest, after we arrived there, I consider as very classified as I have never been debriefed of those activities.

Harvey Walden

I was a West Virginia dairy, horse, and sheep farm boy. At that time, Hitler was trying to take over the world. I wanted to do my part to stop him, so in March 1941, I joined the Army Air Corps and was sent to Jefferson Barracks in St. Louis, Missouri.

On the weekend of December 7, my buddy Paul Beaver was going out with a girl named Mildred Atkins. She had a friend named Fay Werges who wanted to go on a blind date with me because she saw my picture. So I did go on a double date with her and the other couple. I thought Fay was pretty nice. We drove around the countryside and at noon stopped at Elsberry's for a hamburger. While we were in the restaurant, news came on the radio that Pearl Harbor had been attacked by Japan and that all GIs should report back to their camps. We thought we may never see each other again, so we took our good old time getting back to camp. We thought Japan would take over the United States.

I ended up in Saipan, South Pacific, in supply and was discharged in December 1945. I reached the rank of staff sergeant.

Despite the happenings, I did make another date with Fay in three weeks. We were married in 1943 and ended up having three children, five grandchildren, and two great-grandchildren. I lost my wife September 24, 1996. My suspicion was right. She was the prettiest and the nicest woman in the world.

Jim Salisbury

On December 7, 1941, I was a quartermaster third class assigned to the YT 324, a small yard tug. We were stationed at Astoria, Oregon, at the section base. Just the week before, we had painted our tug. It looked good, all clean and smart looking.

Being Sunday, there was not much going on at the section base. A Coast Guard cutter, I think it was the *Algonquin*, was tied astern of us, and it was as quiet as the rest of the base was.

I was in the pilot house, correcting a few charts and manuals, and just hanging around on a lazy Sunday. We were tied up directly across from the administration building. The radio shack was on the second floor and we could easily see into it at high tide.

I heard someone yell at me and I looked out to see a radioman waving at me to come over to the administration building. I figured we had a call to do something. When I got there, he informed me that Pearl Harbor was under attack by Japanese aircraft. I never felt anything like it before or after. I could not believe it.

Within a few minutes all hands knew what was going on. The Coast Guard cutter was alive with men. Everyone seemed lost. What do you do in this case? There was no enemy near you so you just wait for orders from someone.

Those on the cutter began painting its nice white self with battleship gray. I don't know who or where the orders came from, but she was getting ready to go on patrol.

It was a long day. Many of the men at the base had been battleship sailors and had served on the ships at Pearl. They were dumbfounded as the news of the defeat came in from Pearl.

I will never forget that day, nor will I forgive our political leaders for what they allowed to happen to our fleet to get us into the war to help Great Britain. I still remember and always will.

JOHN W. McDONALD

I was stationed at the Naval Air Station Opa Locka in Miami, Florida, on December 7, 1941. I had joined the navy in June 1941. Opa Locka was a naval aviation training base, and we had planes that were older models than those currently operating in the fleet.

I was in the duty section that Sunday and was restricted to the base while our section had the duty. It was early afternoon when the announcement advised that Pearl Harbor had been bombed, and all of the men not on duty were mustered immediately.

All of our airplanes normally were congregated on the ramps. They were all moved away from the hangars and dispersed in the fields so if an attack were to occur, the planes wouldn't be in a concentrated area.

No one at that time had any idea what was happening or if we would be vulnerable to any kind of attack. It turned out that we were not, of course.

When we woke up the next morning, we heard a three-plane section of fighters orbiting over the air station in case of an attack. It was a nice feeling to know that we were somewhat prepared.

After a few days, it was determined that there was not any threat to the naval air station, so training was resumed.

FRANK J. GOUGH

I enlisted on the 7th of November, 1939. I went from Bolling Field in DC to Selfridge Field, Michigan. From there I went to Morrison Field in West Palm Beach.

I was lying on my bunk in my barracks that fatal Sunday noon. I was listening to my radio when the news broke. I was with the 8th Fighter Squadron, 49th Fighter Group. I might add that we were in Australia within forty days. We went to the Northern Territory then to New Guinea.

HERB HEBIG

I was already in the Army on December 7, 1941, because I had received my second lieutenant Functional Areas commission, or F.A., through ROTC at Michigan State. I went on active duty going from Detroit to Camp Livingston, Louisiana. It was a brigade of heavy artillery. I reported in April 1941. I was in the battery officers school at Fort Still, Oklahoma.

While at Camp Livingston, I applied for a transfer to the air force's chemical warfare division because I had a degree in chemical engineering and wanted overseas duty.

I received no replies until Sunday, December 7, 1941. We had a Sunday mail service, and when I picked up my mail I found a red-bordered War Department letter advising me that on or about January 23, 1942, I was to report to the port of San Francisco for transport to the Philippines. I was thrilled over the news until that afternoon. While at a movie, there was an announcement about Pearl Harbor. I was not quite so happy as further news became available.

I was told to ignore the transfer orders and, after my schooling, return to the 46th F.A. Brigade. I didn't think so at the time, but it was a break for me. I spent the next couple of years in Louisiana, then caught a break and was transferred to Third Army HQ Artillery Section at Fort Sam Houston, Texas. From there we were shipped out of New York in March 1944. I was on the Third Army staff with General George S. Patton as the commanding general and traveled from England through the entire European campaign.

I returned to Detroit in October 1945. It was a great experience having served under Patton.

HORACE ROSE

On December 6, 1941, my outfit returned to Camp Blanding, Florida, after spending a month on the Carolina maneuvers. We played soldiers, waving a flag or branch showing we had antitank guns (which we didn't have at the time).

Anyway, we went to sleep that night, dead tired, when some GI came into our tent and shouted that the Japs bombed Pearl Harbor. In unison, practically everyone shouted, "Where the hell is that place?" Unfortunately, it took us three-and-a-half years more to know exactly where it was, but most of us made it back home from the ETO.

HAROLD C. SMITH

On December 7, 1941, I was lying on my cot at Fort McClellan, Alabama, listening to the radio. I was a member of the 165th Infantry Regiment National Guard, federalized on October 15, 1940.

I had bus tickets to go to New York for a three-week Christmas furlough. Instead of New York it became, "California here we come!" I survived as a rifleman in the central Pacific—Makin Island, Saipan, and Okinawa. Pearl Harbor got me for thirty-nine months overseas, no furloughs. The good Lord was with me. God bless those who gave their all.

EDWARD B. REINHARD

I was drafted in June, 1941, and stationed at the New Orleans Army Air Base, a new military camp. I was young and thoroughly enjoyed New Orleans. Any duties were over at 4 p.m. on the weekdays, and we were free from Saturday noon until Monday morning.

On December 7, I was with a date having cocktails and dinner at the Roosevelt Hotel. I didn't know anything about the attack until the taxi driver told us on the way to her home (remember, I was in civilian clothes).

The girl's father was really upset when he opened the door. There were radio spots ordering all military personnel to return to their bases. Also, the movie theaters made similar reports.

I checked in around 10 p.m. and I think I was the last one to report. Luckily my friends knew my usual weekend habits, and I received no reprimand. The group left shortly for Muroc Dry Lake, California, and we arrived there on Christmas Eve.

HOWARD MYERS

I was called into the army selective service in September 1941. I was at Kelly Air Force Base outside of San Antonio, Texas, on December 7, 1941. The news came from the orderly room. They told us, "If you have civilian clothes, send them home or burn them. You're in the Army now."

I was sent all over the country and England during the war. The enemy never attempted to invade our airfield. Their aim was to kill innocent women and children. We were ready for a fight, though.

To break down their morale, Churchill said there would be blood, sweat, and tears—though victory in the end. The 8th Army Air Corps played a major role in the defeat of Hitler.

I was released after four years and two months and came home.

LINCOLN NOE

When I heard that the Japs had bombed Pearl Harbor, it was on a small radio in our medical sleeping quarters in Cheyenne, Wyoming, at Fort Francis E. Warren. I didn't know where Pearl Harbor was. I told 1st Sgt. Charley Caddy. His comment was, "God damn it, we're at war!" He knew of Pearl Harbor.

My group was the 183rd Field Artillery made up from the Idaho National Guard. HQ was originally in Boise, Idaho, as cavalry. My group was a medical attachment to the 183rd. At that time we were planning a Christmas furlough back to Idaho.

The weather that day was clear and cold. This was the day that my wife, Lenora Noe, back in Idaho, gave birth to our first child—a six pound eight ounce boy named Lincoln Richard Noe.

The impact of the happenings of that day was that the army decided to stretch our stay of one year to the duration plus six months. My "year" went from April 1, 1941, to September 30, 1945. Exactly forty-five months later, I finished the war in the South Pacific with Hospital Ship Platoon 945 MHSP.

I also remember when the Japs asked for capitulation after the dropping of the second atomic bomb at Nagasaki in August 1945. I was at an outdoor movie in Manila, Philippines. Every gun on the island was fired into the air. What a sight to behold. I was a medic and had nothing to shoot but my hypodermic needles.

VICTOR PENNER

It was a quiet Sunday afternoon in Camp Joseph T. Robinson, Arkansas. I was in a five-man tent listening to a radio when it came on the air that the Japs had bombed Pearl Harbor. It was hard to believe. Two weeks later, ours, the 35th Division, was at Fort Ord.

I was caught in the first draft February 21, 1941, and sent to Marion, Kansas, to Camp Robinson, Arkansas, and was assigned to Company K, 137th Infantry Regiment of the 35th Division. We made Louisiana maneuvers that summer. We made Tennessee maneuvers for two months starting at Thanksgiving in 1943. We were in England a short time before we went into combat on July 10 and I was wounded on July 31. The division went on for 1,600 combat miles including the Battle of the Bulge. I got a medical discharge on May 19, 1945.

EMMANUEL GLOE

I was at Fort Wood in the army on December 7, 1941. I went in the service on the 3rd of July in 1941. I had been working with the Corps of Engineers in St. Charles when I received a notice from Uncle Sam to join him. Anyway, on Sunday morning we went to church, came back, and had a little dinner, then decided to go to the theater and catch a show. That Sunday was a day off for us.

After the show, we stopped at the PX to get a couple of candy bars because we weren't going to have much of a supper. I was squad leader downstairs and we had a squad leader upstairs. I had a radio, and when I returned to the barracks, somebody hollered down, "We've got your radio up here. Come on up."

I replied, "Oh, I'll be up after a while."

They shot back, "Well, didn't you hear what happened?"

I replied, "No, what happened?"

He answered, "They bombed Pearl Harbor!" We had been at the theater earlier and they didn't even announce it over there.

It wasn't long until the man in charge of quarters came in and wanted the squad leaders to come over to the dayroom because we had to get guards assigned. He told us to pick the best man we had to go on guard and he would be carrying a loaded rifle. A lot of men had trouble getting past the MPs (Military Police) because they had lost their passes. Now those things became very important because everybody had been called back to camp on such short notice.

Our outfit was to train together, stay together, and to fight together for the duration. Some buddies and I served together for four-and-a-half years. Two of them were from the same county I was. We had a lot of them killed and crippled.

We were the 6th Division, 65th Regiment, 63rd Infantry, 3rd Battalion, Company M. We made four beachheads and started up the coast of New Guinea. We didn't see any Red Cross shows. We didn't see any reporters. We saw nothing but war. We rarely saw a cot or had a decent meal. Most people wouldn't believe the life we lived.

On the 30th of March in 1945, I received a shrapnel wound from Japanese artillery. We were in the Philippines protecting the Wawa and Ipo Dams from having the Japanese blow them up. Those furnished water for Manila. I ended up in the hospital for two months. I have thirty inches of scars from that wound. With my calf torn up, the circulation wasn't good and that caused a lot of deterioration to the leg. After that, I was sent back to the same outfit and went right back to combat.

We were in combat the day we heard the war had ended. When we heard the news, they told us to pull back. There was no celebrating because we had been in combat for so long and we were worn out. The only thing we had to celebrate with was our guns. All we had to eat were C rations. They also sent us out a lot of leaky tents. We just sat back and relaxed. We, unfortunately, had a man killed two days after the announcement.

After the war, my brother and I couldn't get a job. There were no Corps of Engineers jobs anymore, so we went and bought 660 acres of productive farmland. We had been raised on a farm. We ended up with a couple of hundred head of cattle. We didn't give much for the land when we bought it but got a lot in return.

7

THE ULTIMATE SACRIFICE

As in any war, there is a great toll on life and property. The estimated cost to world governments during World War II exceeded $1,000,000,000,000.[1] However, no monetary figure can be attached to human suffering. Each death carries a different expense to those left behind.

Still, counting total casualties from World War II is an inexact science. The numbers are a given when recording who did and did not come home from the conflict. It is the whats and wheres of a particular soldier's demise that may never be known.

Depending on which figures are included in a group of statistical data, most tables show that the United States suffered the loss of approximately 292,000 soldiers during World War II.[2] An additional 115,000 soldiers died from noncombat related causes.[3]

Human deaths made up only one type of casualty inflicted by the war. A family could lose a loved one and eventually pass through the standard, yet painful, mourning process of the departed. But what happens when the loss a family or individual suffers is the deprivation of their freedom?

During the war years, Japanese Americans, both native born and immigrants, were no longer free to come and go as they pleased due to nothing they personally brought about. They became prisoners of their own ancestral heritage.

In February 1942, President Roosevelt passed Executive Order 9066, approving the evacuation of all people of Japanese background from the West Coast of the United States.[4] Most were interned in temporary camps until more permanent structures could be constructed. From 1942, through the duration of the war, more than 100,000 Japanese Americans would spend their days behind barbed wire, often enduring harsh weather conditions and insufficient provisions.[5]

Chapter 7 is dedicated to those who suffered the loss of life or liberty after December 7, 1941.

VIVIENNE WILLIAMS

In Rhode Island on December 7, 1941, we had just gotten home from church and turned on the radio. That's when we heard the news. As old as my dad was, he even received a notice to be drafted. He had seven sons and two daughters at the time. My dad had served in the navy in World War I. He swore, until his dying day, that our president knew that Pearl Harbor was coming.

On Monday, my mother went down to the Red Cross and told them she had a son in the navy stationed at Kaneohe Bay, Hawaii. They told her to just go home and wait. "You're not the only one with a son in the Navy you know." My mother wasn't happy with the Red Cross until the day she died.

My nineteen-year-old brother wasn't even supposed to be at Pearl Harbor. John Daniel Buckley was supposed to be on a ship working as an aviation ordnance man. When the bombing started, he was sleeping. His citation stated that he proceeded from the barracks and broke into the ammunition room. He and a friend got out machine guns, and John set his up next to a hangar. His friend set up a bit further away. The hangar was bombed causing it to collapse killing my brother. His friend lived and was able to come home and tell us what happened.

On Wednesday, the brother of a girl my brother was dating had to deliver the telegram stating that John was at Pearl Harbor and was classified as "Missing in Action." He just couldn't bring himself to deliver the telegram. Eddy went to my brother and said, "I have this telegram to deliver." He was on a bicycle at the time. He continued, "I just can't do it. What can I do?"

My brother took the telegram and called my sister, me, and, I believe, my brother Andrew. We all went to the house at the same time and broke the news to Mom and Dad. There was nothing we could do after that but wait. The following Wednesday we finally received official word that he had been killed in action. That's how they notified people of a loss back then. Now they have notification teams.

In 1972, just over thirty years later, I was at Mom and Dad's when the notification team came to tell me of my son Robert. It was on a Sunday, Mother's Day, when the staff car pulled up. My knees started shaking. I recognized the colonel, Red Cross lady, and chaplain, and knew why they were there. After three-and-a-half tours of Vietnam, it was almost expected.

John's remains were returned, but not immediately. We all believed that John was killed instantly until one day mom received his personal effects in what appeared to be a 500-pound crate. Included were two big towels with blood stains on them. Dad was furious.

The first destroyer escort, D.E. 51, was named in my brother's honor. Mom christened the *John D. Buckley*. I still have a piece of the champagne bottle somewhere. After that, all of the destroyer escorts were called the "Buckley Class" after my brother.

My younger brother, who was in boot camp shortly before the ship was christened, wrote to Admiral Nimitz directly, to see if he could get on that ship after boot camp. His wish was granted.

GAYLE TIPSWORD NORRIS

We were a Depression family. We lived on a farm, and at that time we had no electricity, refrigerator, or freezer. We didn't even have a car to drive around in. While we were a poor family, we didn't know we were poor. We had plenty to eat and enough clothes. We were happy and foolish. We though we had everything.

Keith Tipsword was the oldest, my mother's first child. He and my mother were very close. After seeing very little future in our area, he joined the navy in 1939. Keith was aboard the *West Virginia* stationed at Pearl Harbor. He knew we'd soon be at war. He said, "If I get out, get married, or get a good job and they call me back, it will disrupt my whole life. I don't want that to happen so I'll stay in for now. Maybe in two years time it will all be over and I can get out and stay out."

On December 7th, I was on a train from Houston going back home to Effingham, Illinois. I had my girl with me as she was just two years old. We had to walk through the club car to the diner. There was a lady who seemed receptive to conversation so I asked, "What's going on the radio?"

She said, "Oh, the Japanese have bombed Pearl Harbor."

I said, "Oh, I have a brother there on the *West Virginia*."

As long as we were on that train, nobody else mentioned anything more about the news. When we got to Effingham, I left the bags at the station and walked, carrying my daughter, to my parents' home. I couldn't wait to get there to find out what they'd heard. Well, they hadn't heard anything at that time.

My mother and all of us couldn't believe that he wouldn't be O.K. Nell, my brother's girlfriend, sent a telegram to my mother saying that Keith would be alright. Then my parents got a telegram that said, after an extensive search had been made and his body still hadn't been recovered, Keith was declared missing in action.

The telegraph office here was only open during the day at that time, so the man who worked the railroad tower took incoming telegrams through the night. He called the house and asked Dad if he should deliver the telegram or read it to him. Dad said, "Read it."

"After an extensive search, it has been found impossible to locate your son, Keith Warren Tipsword, Machinist Mate, First Class, United States Navy, and he has therefore been officially declared to have lost his life in the service of his country as of December 7, 1941. The Department expresses to you its sincerest sympathy. —Rear Admiral Randall Jacobs, Chief of Bureau of Navigation, Washington, DC."

Before the war, you wanted to get a telegram. It was sort of a treat, something special. After the war started, nobody wanted a telegram. Just the fact that you got one was bad news. You didn't want to read it, didn't want to know what it said because most of them bore bad news.

AMY ESTES

Around that time I was in my early teens. Dad had invited our visiting minister home for Sunday dinner and my mother had sent me to our regular minister's home to borrow something. They had their radio on, but I was not listening to it when he told me to run home and tell my dad to turn on our radio. Not realizing why, I ran home, gave my mother what I had been sent after, and went straight to our radio and turned it on. Then I turned to my dad. His face, the face of our visiting minister, and the crash of the dish my mother dropped made me listen and hear what was being said. I'll never forget the look on my parents' faces.

I grew up at that moment, as I had two brothers in the National Guard who had just departed for Pearl Harbor. They helped clean up the harbor.

Another brother wanted to enlist but we talked him out of it. None of us felt he would be accepted. His trigger finger was missing and another on the same hand was cracked. He told us he would be drafted and sent to the other side of the war and might never see his brothers again. He was right. He went to Africa, Anzio Beach, then into Germany where he lost his life. I was called home from college to be with my mother after she received the notice of his death.

The other brothers went all the way to Japan then came back home safe and whole in body. I was home when she received the telegram from the first of my other brothers who returned home. She had been alone when the telegram came, telling her of the loss of her son before, and was just beginning to live again when this telegram came. She wouldn't open it. She came to me and I had to open it and give her the good news.

Dorothy Wiese Ferreira

I was just thirteen at the time. My sister and I were at my grandparents for Sunday dinner. Dad got us one day a week for visitation. All of us had finished eating—my dad, my aunt, both grandparents, my new stepmom (who I adored), my sister who is four years younger, and myself. I was laying on the floor with my head under the radio and just playing around when my grandfather said for everyone to be quiet and listen. I went and sat on my dad's lap and you could hear a pin drop. Things just progressed from there.

We lived thirteen miles from Fort Dix in Trenton, New Jersey, and things began to happen. Every newsreel in the movies was full of war news and posters went up very quickly. We had already seen the news from Europe with Hitler's doings, so it became the topic of conversation everywhere. In fact a few years later, I got the first "A" I ever received in art class in the 10th grade. I did an India ink drawing of Hitler, with some sort of slogan I made up (I can't recall what it said), and it was displayed at school. I remember I used a fifty cent piece to draw the head of Hitler. The poster itself was plain, but to the point.

Then our high school buddies started talking about joining up, and many of them did. I remember vividly the ones that did not return. One was Victor who joined the navy and went down with his ship in the South Pacific. Another was Maurice who went into the army and was sent to Europe where he was killed in France I believe. There are a few more, and I get teary-eyed thinking about them. Our group wrote to many of them.

I also had a pen pal in England, and her brother was in the military as well. We exchanged pictures, but eventually lost track of each other.

At age sixteen, I became engaged to a serviceman. He went to Italy and was wounded there.

When I was married the last time, also to a vet, we became very active in the VFW (Veterans of Foreign Wars). People need to know what a vet is and to stay aware of what they did for us. Without their sacrifices, we would not have the freedoms we take for granted today.

Maggy Buchanan

I do remember that I had just come out of a neighborhood theater after seeing a matinee, and people were talking about Japan bombing Pearl Harbor. My oldest brother was already in the air force. I almost ran home to hear the news on the radio.

My youngest brother enlisted in the Marine Corps and left right after graduation from high school. He fought in the Pacific and was awarded a Purple Heart.

My mother worked in a manufacturing plant making bomb parts and my father was a city fireman.

Two of my best friends were killed in the invasion of Salerno. One had been married just a few months and the other was his brother-in-law. They were killed within just two days of each other.

DOVIE RUBY

I was living in Detroit, Michigan, when I heard the news that Pearl Harbor was bombed. My husband and I were driving to visit a family member and heard it on the car radio.

We immediately called my husband's best buddy and his wife. We were all shocked, angry, and frightened of what it could do to everyone's lives.

My husband was stationed in the navy, St. Petersburg, Florida, and Miami. In San Juan, Puerto Rico, he developed cancer and passed away at the naval hospital in New York, in May of 1947. I later remarried.

LUCILLE DEAN

I was living in a small town, Henryville, Indiana. I was living with Mr. and Mrs. Clifford Collings, caring for their three daughters. They were both working.

This day I had gone to church, and as the Collings were gone, I was alone until mid-afternoon. I had started to walk to Furnish's Restaurant where young people met. On the way I met my friend Barbara Costin. She was crying. She told me about Pearl Harbor. Her brother, "Buddie," and our friend Howard Prall, were at Pearl Harbor.

Buddie Costin was killed on the USS *Virginia*. Howard Prall, if I remember correctly, was on the USS *Maryland*. He was only wounded. This was a bad time for the people of Henryville, for these two men were much loved by all.

Just a few years ago, Buddie's personal belongings were sent to his sister at Henryville.

ELINOR DOWNS, M.D.

I remember December 7, 1941, as marking a major turning point in my life. During the years 1939–40, before Pearl Harbor, my husband Roge and I were deeply absorbed in our final period of training as physicians. We were young, very much in love, hoping to soon start a family, and thinking, with anticipation, about our future career plans. We were hardly aware of the distant turmoil in Europe or the Far East. Our picture of those events was hazy, dependent entirely upon newspaper accounts and radio broadcasts, which seemed almost unreal-faraway occurrences.

We knew that the government in Washington, while sending non military aid to beleaguered European nations, was officially "strictly neutral." President Roosevelt was promising over and over that the United States would not become militarily involved and that "our boys will never again be sent to wars overseas." We felt protected, immune from danger. Somehow, the realities of what was happening abroad, nor the immediacy of war, really dawned on us or those associated with us.

By 1941, full of enthusiasm, Roge and I were ready to start out on our own. We had decided to set up a joint medical practice somewhere in New England. After months of searching, we finally settled on a beautiful, small, historic town in northwest Connecticut, and looked forward to the move.

In September of that year, for $50 a month, we rented a compact colonial saltbox-style house located near the center of the village. Taking out a bank loan, and with the owner's permission, we modified one section of the house into a small but efficient office and laboratory. Before the ground froze, we dug a hole in the front lawn near the sidewalk and "planted" a sturdy white post from which to hang our double M.D. shingle.

By December, not only were we ready to start our professional venture, we were also rejoicing in the knowledge that our second child would be arriving in about six months.

Thus, in high spirits and hopes, on the crisp Sunday afternoon of December 7, 1941, we set out on foot to make brief courtesy calls on the other three participating physicians in town, all of whom had graciously wished us well. It was a heartwarming afternoon!

Upon returning home around 5 p.m., we flipped on the radio and heard the astounding news—a surprise attack on Pearl Harbor! Within hours the United States was at war with Japan in the Pacific, and six days later, with Germany and Italy in Europe!

None of us knew just what being at war would mean, or how it would affect our lives. Although stunned and shocked, Roge and I tried at first to carry on as normally as possible. Patients began to appear at the office, or call, and Christmas was in the air. But life was not "as usual." Subtle and not-so-subtle changes and pressures we couldn't anticipate or control slowly closed in around us all. More and more our family lived from day to day, not thinking or planning beyond June when the baby was due.

We watched as able-bodied and nonessential men from our village, as from all small New England towns, were drafted into the armed services. Able-bodied women drifted into industrial and munitions plants in nearby cities. The town's dwindling population pulled together in patriotic support by establishing first aid centers and Red Cross classes, collecting scrap metal, conducting war bond drives, manning airplane spotting stations, and serving as air wardens. Evacuation and refugee housing plans were debated and CARE packages were assembled. We learned to stand patiently in line at food counters and spend our ration stamps carefully. We painted the top half of our headlights black, and when the practice air-raid sirens wailed at night and the town blacked out, we dutifully descended to our basement family room without windows until the all clear signal sounded. Like everyone else, we became participants in the war effort as we tried to come to reasonable terms with what was changing so rapidly all around us.

By March 1942, three months after Pearl Harbor, it became clear that if Roge didn't make concrete decisions about military service, they would be made for him. As a physician, he was too new to the community to be declared "essential," and as a thirty-one-year-old able-bodied male, even with a family, he was in a high priority army draft category. I don't think it ever occurred to either of us or our families that Roge would not eventually serve, but he wanted time to see his new baby and to be sure his family would be cared for while he was away.

Our bouncing son arrived on schedule in June, and in July Roge volunteered in the navy. His commission in the Navy Medical Corps arrived in September, and he executed the oath of office on October 3, 1942—ten months after Pearl Harbor. From that date, his comings and goings were controlled entirely by the navy. He never really came home again to stay. Following a six-month training stint in submarine and deep-sea diving medicine in Washington and New York, he was shipped out of the country. He spent almost two years in the Mediterranean on a salvage ship.

As a medical officer, his responsibility was to care for the underwater divers who cleared captured harbors, from North Africa to Italy, of explosives and debris.

Roge died in service in February 1945, a little over four years after Pearl Harbor. I closed the office, took down our shingle, and left our lovely country practice to enter academic medicine, moving with our two children to start a new life in "the big city."

JOHN Y. HAYAKAWA

To begin with, I was renting acreage in the floodplain north of the city of San Jose. For a quick cash crop I planted market cucumbers in the spring for harvest in late June. In the interim, I concentrated on transplanting celery plants from the seed beds to watered furrows. This crop required a lot of fertilization and furrow cultivation to stimulate growth of the large heads of celery as it was priced by the crate.

On December 7, 1941, I had finished a very profitable harvest in October. Orders were flowing in for the holiday season. It was just a matter of filling orders at that point.

That Sunday, as we were packing for Monday market, we ran out of crate covers. I got in the car to go to our supplier to pick up more covers. On the way to town I turned on the radio and there it was: Pearl Harbor bombed.

I purchased our covers and went back to the farm. I informed my parents of the emergency. They asked me what I was going to do. I told them to finish filling the orders and I would take the celery to market as I had promised. It did not occur to me the gravity of the situation even though I was twenty-three-years-old. I did not panic.

With the war on our minds, we were waiting for the other shoe to drop. Between rains, we took our time cleaning up the fields after the harvest.

I do not remember when *The Japanese Vernacular* discontinued publication, but my parents had nothing left to read but old Japanese magazines. Our only source of information was the morning *San Jose Mercury Herald* and eventually the postings on utility poles.

The Department of Justice in San Francisco issued a proclamation that all Japanese and all Americans of Japanese ancestry shall not travel beyond a five-mile perimeter of their home. My parents decided not to visit friends, or even go shopping to Japantown in San Jose. Most correspondence was done by mail—especially about rumors.

The United States Department of Justice stated that all aliens apply for and be issued a certificate of identification. On it was recorded the alien registration number, fingerprint, photo, signature, date and place of birth, origin of citizenry in the United States, mailing address, height, weight, and color of hair.

My parents were issued their certificate of identification signed and dated on February 8, 1942. This was to be their passport forever after. On any official business they were asked to always present the now famous "pink book."

February 19, 1942, came Executive Order 9066. It authorized the establishment of military areas and the exclusion therefrom of "any and all persons." The army proclamation made clear that not only aliens but also an American born of Japanese ancestry would be affected. The restricted military areas were defined as the western halves of the Pacific Coast states. We were now under the jurisdiction of the army.

Since the facilities were limited, for those who desired, permission was granted to voluntarily move inland at their own expense. Because of the many disappointments at attempting to qualify for such a trek, many decided to take their chances at the mandatory evacuation. My parents decided it was best to go as a group.

I had a lady friend that I was seriously intending to go beyond friendship. I visited her many times as did my parents. One morning I was called to the phone because my lady friend's brother wanted to speak with me.

"John, the FBI just took our father," he said. "I don't know what to do. My mother told me to at least let you know."

The father/husband was the only one detained in all of Santa Clara County. He was a hard working and successful farmer who was a legally registered Japanese alien. No mention was made as to why he was arrested. The mother was strong in her sudden burden of responsibility, abruptly a single parent of four daughters and a son.

Later the family was told that the family head was detained and confined at Sharp Park Military Facility near the Pacific Ocean. Eventually, permission was granted that family members "only" visit. He was later transferred to military confinement at Bismark, North Dakota, before ending up in Lordsburg, New Mexico.

One afternoon I was called to the phone and the caller introduced himself as Louis B. Wine, FBI agent. He asked if I knew a Mrs. Yamada. I told him that she taught Japanese language in Evendale. He asked if I could tell him of her conducting any un-American or anti-American activities. I said I did not know as I had never enrolled in any of her language classes. Mr. Wine's closing remarks were that I was a poor representative of the Citizen's League for not reporting any enemy alien activities. The league's president said that I handled the situation very well by telling the truth.

Finally the other shoe dropped. On the way to the office, I saw posted on a utility pole the following: All Persons Of Japanese Ancestry, Both Alien And Non-Alien, Report To The San Jose State College Men's Gymnasium For Registration And Issuance Of A Family Number In Preparation For Evacuation.

I was asked to assist in the registration, especially with the non-English-speaking generation. I told my lady friend to register on the day before me so that we would be sent to the same camp. We were to be notified by mail the where and when.

Our landlord told us we'd be home in six months, so for us to isolate one room in our house, put all of our things in there, and he'd keep an eye on it.

I sold the two tractors, horse, and two trucks for a decent price. I made arrangements for storage of the family's 1940 car.

Finally, departure notices were printed in the newspaper. Official notices were issued by mail. We/all were informed to report to the Southern Pacific Station in San Jose at the assigned departure date and time.

Our destination was the Santa Anita Racetrack in Pasadena, California (named WCCA Santa Anita Assembly Center).

Departures began in mid-April in groups of about 500 people in each movement. Every week, trainloads departed. On the next-to-last trainload (ours), I was informed by my lady friend that their family was rerouted to the Pamona County Fair Grounds since Santa Anita wasn't yet ready to receive its 500 people that week.

I went to my lady friend's home and took the family to the departure center. In parting, her mother gave me an envelope. The message read: "Thank you for everything you have done for us. Please be patient. Under the circumstances, I cannot make any promises and I know you do not expect me to. Take care of yourself and your parents. Someday blossoms will bloom in Spring and good things may happen. Sayonara, Mother."

Finally, the last contingent (us) went to the train station for departure. We being last, there were no friends to see us off.

On the train ride south, I had a lot of things on my mind—especially my lady friend. The MPs were high profile at the start of the trip, so I did not sneak a peek under the drawn shades.

The train made a long stop at Watsonville, reportedly to disembark one of the passengers who had drowned his sorrow with too much drink and had poisoned himself.

I was able to sneak a peek later on a couple of occasions. Once I saw the oil derricks of Long Beach bathed in moonlight. Another time we were at the rail yards at the Los Angeles Freight Terminal. I saw a news vending machine carrying the headline "John Barrymore Has Died." It was May 29, 1942—My lady friend's birthday. Happy Birthday, wherever you are, I thought.

My family stayed at the Santa Anita Assembly Center. I contributed to the war effort by weaving camouflage patterns into netting at $12 a month. I corresponded to my lady friend by mail. Her replies helped me keep my sanity. Finally, one of her letters in August of 1942 told me that her family was destined to Heart Mountain War Relocation Center in Park County, Wyoming.

In September 1942, we were issued official confirmation that most all contingencies that departed from San Jose were also destined for Heart Mountain. The intent was to keep the community together. I was elated.

As we rode the trains towards our destination, I saw the cultured palm tree orchards of Palm Springs at dusk. We went through Yuma, Arizona; Lordsburg, New Mexico; Crystal City, Texas; Denver, Colorado; Casper, Wyoming; then finally to Heart Mountain in the middle of the night.

Somewhere in that city of 10,000 sleeping was my lady friend whom I hadn't seen in nearly four months.

On October 9, 1943, my lady friend and myself were united in marriage conducted by Justice of the Peace W. S. Owen Jr. at his home in Cody, Wyoming.

In August 1943, my son was born in Heart Mountain, Wyoming.

In May 1999, for the first time in fifty-seven years, I invited my son (camp souvenir) to return with me to Heart Mountain. I wanted to show him where he was born. Also, friends who visited the site told me of the still-existing high school concrete storage vault. Our honeymoon apartment was west of the football field. I wanted to visit my former home site, using the vault as a beginning.

Upon arrival, I was flooded with memories upon seeing the camp site minus the rows of barracks. The county road ran west, adjacent to the high school vault. A half a block down the road stood this magnificent Poplar/Cottonwood, standing stately over 150 feet high. It is the only living thing in the whole 750 remaining acres. I was amazed it had survived the hazards of nature and mankind all of these years. I had planted this sapling many years ago in front of our honeymoon apartment (I took a picture of it when I planted it). No one lives on the site.

As of this writing, I am eighty-one-years-old. My spouse and I celebrated our fifty-fifth wedding anniversary on October 9, 1998.

MARY YOSHIDA

I am a Japanese American born in Central Point, Oregon. I was a freshman at Oregon State College at the time. I was living in a home while attending school. I was serving breakfast to the lady of the house when she told me to stop and listen to the radio. That is how I found out about the news.

I was not able to complete my freshman year because I was ordered to report to an American concentration camp in Tule Lake, California. My sister and I were split up because she was in school in Seattle. She ended up in Minidoka, a camp in Idaho. We eventually joined back up in Minnesota afterwards. There were over 110,000 Japanese and Japanese Americans put behind barbed wire for the duration of the war.

I later graduated from Texas Wesleyan College with a B.A. in Religious Education.

PETER YOSHIDA, M.D.

I was a young fellow, about seven years of age, so the impact of the attack wasn't what it was to my parents. We were in church when the news came about. Because we were in church, we didn't hear that we had to get out of the West Coast. They gave us only four days to close up our affairs and pack up. We were only allowed one suitcase per person.

My father was a fairly large farmer in California. He actually came to the United States as a schoolteacher. He was going to take some studies in San Francisco, then go back to teach in Tokyo at a business school. But since his father died, and with him being the oldest, the whole family relocated to San Francisco. His father was starting to make a living doing some farming, so my father got in on that end of it. He ended up with a pretty large farm with not only vegetables but also fruit to ship back east.

When we had to leave in such a hurry, and people knew we had to leave, they didn't come by and ask, "How much?" referring to a price for our property, equipment, tools, etc. Friends, or those we thought were friends, came by with their trucks and asked, "What can I have?" referring to refrigerators and stuff like that. We gave away everything, basically. That hurt my father, I think. He had lots of farming equipment and just had to give it all away. It was either that or they would have taken it away after we left anyway. Also, our crops were fairly close to harvest but there was little we could do about that.

The furniture that we had, like beds and other household furnishings, we stored at the Japanese church in Mountain View (California). It was located on what is now Alma Expressway and Shoreline. All of the church members brought in their own furniture, stored it, boarded up the door, the windows and everything.

When we were made to leave in December of 1941, I don't think our parents knew where we were going. We ended up in a holding area in Santa Anita—the race track. Some people stayed in the horse's stalls. They just cleared it out and whitewashed it. For the rest of us, they made a makeshift type of barracks with everybody sleeping in one room. The slots in the dividers were spaced so that you could see everything that was going on next door. We later put newspaper and things there for a little more privacy.

We had a central toilet and place for washing. When we arrived, we were given sewn sheets. There was hay in the streets, so we basically had to make our own mattress. Some people did this at night and really couldn't see what they were doing. Later while laying there, they could feel something moving around in their mattress. When they investigated, they found that there were snakes living in there.

We had a mess hall where they fed us. We were vegetarians so we kind of struggled with that. It was either that or survive on nothing.

We were later relocated to the mountains outside of Cody, Wyoming. We traveled by train and had to keep the blinds down on the windows so we couldn't see where we were being taken. They said it was for our own protection. If outsiders saw who was on the train, they might shoot at us. We usually only traveled at night and parked the train in the mountains during the day.

In that mountain camp, it got down to thirty to sixty degrees below zero in the winter. I guess they didn't want us near any civilization. Our camp was surrounded by barbed wire and spotlights. The soldiers guarding us were ordered to shoot if we even tried to retrieve a ball outside the fence. It was not a friendly, enjoyable situation.

After the war, we went back to San Francisco. We went to the Japanese church to retrieve our furniture and found that people had pried open the building and looted all of the contents. As a result, we had nothing. Everything we owned was gone except the suitcases we were allowed to take with us.

We stayed at the church on Post Street until my father found a job. We all worked and pooled our money as a family to buy a car or house to establish ourselves.

Having seen our parent's hardships, all of my siblings felt the only way to get ahead was through education. As a result, we all became professionals. We became engineers, dentists, and doctors. We didn't want endure what our parent's had to go through to get ahead in life.

While some people harbored resentment about all of this, I didn't. I was young and was told, "War is war." I did, however, wonder why we were singled out. "What about the German-Americans?" I thought.

NOTES

INTRODUCTION

1. Janet Podell and Steven Anzovin, *Speeches of the American Presidents* (New York: H.W. Wilson Co., 1988), 512–13.
2. *USA Today Weekend*, "Stories of the Century," December 24–26, 1999, 10.

Chapter 1. EYEWITNESS TO TRAGEDY

1. *The New Encyclopedia Britannica*, 15th ed., vol. 29 (Chicago, IL, 1998), 1000.
2. Bureau of the Census, *Historical Statistics of the United States* (Washington, DC: United States Government Printing Office, 1975), 26.
3. Donald M. Goldstein, Katherine V. Dillon, and Michael J. Wenger, *The Way It Was: Pearl Harbor* (Washington, DC, London, and England: Brassey's Trade Paperback Edition, 1995), 19.
4. Ibid.
5. Ibid., 30.

Chapter 2. IMPRESSIONABLE YOUTH

1. Bureau of the Census, *Historical Statistics of the United States* (Washington, DC: United States Government Printing Office, 1975), 10.
2. Ibid., 12.
3. Sheila Rowbotham, *A Century of Women* (New York: Penguin Books USA, 1997), 262.

Chapter 3. HOLDING DOWN THE HOMEFRONT

1. Sheila Rowbotham, *A Century of Women* (New York: Penguin Books USA, 1997), 252.
2. Ibid.

Chapter 4. IN THE LOWER 48

1. Bureau of the Census, *Historical Statistics of the United States* (Washington, DC: United States Government Printing Office, 1975), 8.
2. George Thomas Kurian, *Datapedia of the United States 1790–2000* (Lanham, MD: Bernan Press, 1994), 11.
3. Ibid., 41.
4. Ibid., 79.
5. Ibid.
6. Ibid., 89.
7. Ibid., 129.
8. Ibid., 275.
9. Ibid., 303.
10. Bureau of the Census, *Historical Statistics of the United States* (Washington, DC: United States Government Printing Office, 1975), 783.
11. *Datapedia*, 299.

Chapter 5. ANSWERING THE CALL

1. Bureau of the Census, *Historical Statistics of the United States* (Washington, DC: United States Government Printing Office, 1975), 1141.
2. Ibid., 1143.
3. Ibid.
4. *The New Encyclopedia Britannica*, 15th ed., vol. 29 (Chicago, IL, 1998), 998.
5. Ibid., 1000.
6. Ibid.

Chapter 7. THE ULTIMATE SACRIFICE

1. *The New Encyclopedia Britannica*, 15th ed., vol. 29 (Chicago, IL, 1998), 1023.
2. Ibid.
3. Ibid.
4. David K. Fremon, *Japanese-American Internment in American History* (Springfield, NJ: Enslow Publishing Inc., 1996), 31.
5. Roger Daniels, *Prisoners Without Trial* (New York: Hill and Wang, 1993), 72.

INDEX

About the Editor

K. D. RICHARDSON is a freelance researcher and writer. He is a sports photographer and columnist for *The Venice Cornerstone*.